THE REAL HISTORY OF
ANCIENT EGYPT

J S Thomas

Order this book online at www.trafford.com/08-0986
or email orders@trafford.com

Most Trafford titles are also available at major online book retailers.

© Copyright 2009 Joseph S Thomas.
All rights reserved. No part of this publication may be reproduced, stored in a retrieval system, or transmitted, in any form or by any means, electronic, mechanical, photocopying, recording, or otherwise, without the written prior permission of the author.

Note for Librarians: A cataloguing record for this book is available from Library and Archives Canada at www.collectionscanada.ca/amicus/index-e.html

Printed in Victoria, BC, Canada.

ISBN: 978-1-4251-8461-2

We at Trafford believe that it is the responsibility of us all, as both individuals and corporations, to make choices that are environmentally and socially sound. You, in turn, are supporting this responsible conduct each time you purchase a Trafford book, or make use of our publishing services. To find out how you are helping, please visit www.trafford.com/responsiblepublishing.html

Our mission is to efficiently provide the world's finest, most comprehensive book publishing service, enabling every author to experience success. To find out how to publish your book, your way, and have it available worldwide, visit us online at www.trafford.com/10510

 www.trafford.com

North America & international
toll-free: 1 888 232 4444 (USA & Canada)
phone: 250 383 6864 ♦ fax: 250 383 6804 ♦ email: info@trafford.com

The United Kingdom & Europe
phone: +44 (0)1865 487 395 ♦ local rate: 0845 230 9601
facsimile: +44 (0)1865 481 507 ♦ email: info.uk@trafford.com

10 9 8 7 6 5 4 3

CONTENTS

Foreword	5
Introduction	7
Chapter One. The Real Sothic Cycle	22
Chapter Two. The Exodus	29
Chapter Three. Dynasties 1 and 2 are the Judges	33
Chapter Four. Cheops is Solomon	50
Chapter Five. Diodorus Siculus Gets Cheops Right	56
Chapter Six. The Real Ramses	63
Chapter Seven. The Antonines of the 18th Dynasty	73
Chapter Eight. The Pseudo Antonines of the 18th Dynasty	83
Chapter Nine. Ramses II is Constantine	93
Chapter Ten. The Empire Era Hittites are the Sassanides	102
Chapter Eleven. Ramses III is Theodosius	108
Chapter Twelve. A Chronological Table	117

FOREWORD

IN THIS BRIEF OUTLINE OF THE HISTORY OF EGYPT, I show that the Egyptologists put the earlier dynasties 1600 years too far back and when this mistake is corrected it is obvious that Dynasties 1 through 6 can only be the Kingdom of Israel, while Dynasties 7 through 25 are the successive empires on the Nile of Babylon, Persia, Greece and Rome. I prove this by showing that the men and events of those dynasties match up with the men and events and dynasties of biblical and classical history. But you will be the judge of that, whether I actually do prove it or not. At some point along in these pages you will either agree with me or decide that all I've managed to do is demonstrate what the old saw means that history repeats itself.

Of course, if the Nile Valley was the Promised Land, it could not have been the land of the captivity. In a second book I will show that the biblical Misraim, the name which is translated as Egypt in our Bible, was in fact Musri in Mesopotamia where Sargon I of Akkad was the historical Moses. In this second book I also put the Sumerian King List on the time scale where it belongs to show that it features many familiar figures. The chronologies of the various countries of the Near East are keyed to that of Egypt so that as it is corrected so are they.

The dates I use for biblical history and the old king lists almost always differ from conventional dates. The reason for that is that I use the Bible's own chronology as closely as I can make it and, so far as I can see, it is the same or very nearly the same as that of the old rabbis, Josephus and the early Church fathers. The advantage of course is that it is more accurate. For instance, it starts King David early in 1089 while the usual date is 1010 BC. In another book I'll explain how I discovered it and how it works.

It was not an interest in Egyptian history that started me out on all this but rather the question of where the archaeological evidence for the old Israel had ever gotten off to. As you will see in the following pages answering that question properly leads very quickly to the Nile Valley.

INTRODUCTION

ACCORDING TO THE BIBLE ITSELF, ISRAEL LASTED 919 years from the Exodus in 1519 to the destruction of Jerusalem in 600 BC. For most of that time, its population was several millions and it could put hundreds of thousands of men on the battlefield as a major power. In the reigns of David and Solomon it was the greatest and wealthiest power in the Near East and most likely in the world. Its building programs under Solomon stunned its neighbors. The land it called home was large and fertile and out of the way, hidden, not easily accessible. And there were rivers there.

If we set the Bible at true, take it at its word, the tradition of Palestine has to go because the description of that country is the opposite of the Bible's description of the Promised Land. Palestine has no rivers; it is in the way not out of the way; its soil is poor not fertile; it is small not large; and it has always been this way. Furthermore, it is excluded because archaeology has shown that it never was the home of a major power, Israel's or anyone else's. And sure enough, no archaeologist has ever dug up anything in Palestine and proven it to come from the Kingdom of Israel. No grave, body, foundation, earthwork, woodwork, stonework, King List, text, monument, tool, weapon or utensil, nothing, has ever been found in Palestine and proven to come from that kingdom. All supposed evidence is based on nothing more than guesswork and wishful thinking. All those pages in history books that go on about King David's relations with the 21st Dynasty of Egypt are nothing more than creative writing for the simple reason that there is no evidence for it.

The absence of evidence is why some say that God has banished from the Earth all trace of His rebellious people. It is why the historians discount the Bible story. They say the Kingdom was so small that it was insignificant. But where is their evidence for that? There isn't any. There is none in Palestine to show it was great, but then there is none to show it was small either. No evidence is no evidence either way. If we confine ourselves to Palestine, as though the tradition of that place is more trustworthy than scripture itself, then the only conclusion to be drawn is that the Kingdom never existed, which is absurd. So the only choice we have is to look somewhere outside Palestine. Now, where would that be?

The easiest way to discover where Old Israel called home is to look and see where circumcised mummies come from. Nobody can deny that circumcision had something to do with Israel's identity and religion. They come from Egypt, not from Palestine. In Egypt, circumcised mummies occurred in such millions, them and their contemporary females, that in the 19th century they were only so much biomass to be mined as fertilizer in a traffic reaching Europe and the British Isles. The better specimens went to museums and to the drawing rooms of the wealthy where unwrapping one provided an evening's entertainment. A quack medicine was concocted from mummies and sold as an elixir. Meanwhile, I cannot remember a single instance of a circumcised body dug up in Palestine and proven to come from before the fall of Jerusalem. So, Egypt it is. Obviously this means the land of the captivity was elsewhere.

But now the Egyptologists have a problem. Their Dynasties 18 through 25 that they put in the time of the judges and kings of Israel don't read like the Bible story at all. How does that happen! I haven't missed a step so far. They have. Those dynasties should remind us of Israel but they don't. This can only mean one thing – the Egyptologists have got their chronology wrong. Those dynasties don't belong there on the timescale where they put them. And so there is only one thing to do and that is ignore their chronology and just go looking back until something familiar shows up whatever the date is that is tacked on to it. Here again, there is an easy way to do this – just follow the circumcised bodies.

Grimal, in his 1994 *A History of Ancient Egypt*, says that Egyptology did not get going until it was freed from the 'constraints of biblical limitations'. He doesn't say what those are so let me mention one of them – Israel was the first nation in history to practice circumcision. Nobody did that before. Moses commanded that the people shall not, on pain of death, borrow anything from their neighbors having to do with their, Israel's, identity and religion. Circumcision was Israel's brand. No rancher brands his cattle with his neighbor's mark and neither did they.

Abraham and his men were the first in history to be circumcised which was in 1928 BC. And Israel under Joshua in 1480 BC was the first nation holding territory to practice circumcision. That is the biblical limitation and it serves perfectly well as a constraint on Egyptology. This constraint means that as soon as circumcised bodies first show up in the archaeology of Egypt, the dynasty those bodies belong to will necessarily be Israel and Joshua with the start date of 1480 BC. No hemming and hawing about. That is that. And guess what? The first circumcised mummies come from the 1st Dynasty. None are found from pre-dynastic times.

As a matter of fact, most of those mummies that were mined for fertilizer come from the first six dynasties which were all one nation and such a job was made of it that it is not easy to find any more. Apparently every last soul of them tried to be buried on certain grounds, burial grounds, which made it easy for the miners. This situation was predicted a long time ago. It was an Old Testament prophet who said that their bodies would be cast up to the light of day and go for dung of the field.

So Egypt it is and the first six dynasties are it. Grimal runs these from 3150 to 2200 BC or ten years later, the end of a certain Nitocris ending the 6th Dynasty. That's unconstrained Egyptology for you. In fact, those dynasties run from 1480 BC to the end of the one and only Nitocris in 589 BC which is ten years after the destruction of Jerusalem. She was the daughter of Psammetichus who started his dynasty around 664 BC having been made satrap by the Assyrians who had long since taken Samaria captive.

The first six dynasties lasted for about 900 years. It was Israel from Joshua to Nitocris that lasted that long. These dynasties are divided by the Egyptologists in two: the first two dynasties, the Thinite Period, lasting about 400 years to end with the first ruler to be named King; and the next four dynasties, the Old Kingdom, the time of empire and kings, lasting about 500 years. It was Israel that spent about 400 years under the judges, a time ended by Saul, the first ruler to be King, and then about 500 years under king and empire.

In the 2nd Dynasty is the name Per Ibsen. That's Egyptian for the great gentleman Ibsen. He was only the first among equals. That will be judge Ibsen of Israel.

INTRODUCTION

Starting the 3rd Dynasty and the era of kings and empire after an obscure three years or so is the name Djoser. That's Jasher in the Old Testament, a name for King David who started the era of empire after a three year civil war. Ending this dynasty or starting the 4th, is the name Sneferu. That's Asnapper in the book of Ezra. Asnaffer, Snafferu, Sneferu, it's all the same. The historians don't know who Asnapper is. They guess at the Assyrian Asherbanipal who made Psammetichus satrap. They're wrong. It is Solomon. Imhotep the prince and wise man, Sneferu, and Cheops, are all names of Solomon at various stages of his eighty year career. The old rabbis said he had many names and Josephus said he reigned eighty years, the first seventeen with his father. The Bible mentions his first forty as good years but dismisses his second forty as the time he went bad, as Cheops the cruel taskmaster.

With the death of Cheops the royal house was divided says Grimal. That's right. At the death of Solomon, the ruling house and the country was divided between Jereboam, Solomon's right hand man, and Rehoboam, Solomon's son. Rehoboam drove the country to this because he answered a delegation that while his father used an ordinary whip, he would use one styled the scorpion. And so the ten tribes and all those indigenes living amongst them rebelled. But here, the Egyptologists make their first significant mistake in their relative chronology – they stack the 5th Dynasty on the end of the 4th, when in fact the two ran side by side, the result of the division.

The 4th Dynasty is properly begun by Chephren, Jereboam, not Cheops. The identity of the 5th Dynasty is revealed by the name Asa occurring there. That's King Asa, the great-grandson of Solomon. So the 5th is properly started by Rehoboam but the Egyptologists can't start it with the son of Cheops since they stack this dynasty on the end of the 4th, so they start the Fifth Dynasty with an unknown who is in fact none other than the Bible's Shishak, King of Musri in Mesopotamia. He invaded Egypt and the Kingdom of Judah in the fifth year of Rehoboam.

Grimal names Wenis and Isesi as ending the 5th Dynasty. He does not recognize that these two are Unis and Isses named by Manetho as the last two of the major Hyksos. Manetho does not bother to name the minor Hyksos, the last of whom is Nitocris ending the 6th Dynasty. The Egyptologists do not recognize any Hyksos, foreign overlords, in the Old Kingdom, Dynasties 3 through 6, because for reasons of their own they want to put them in Dynasties 15 and 16. Nitocris was Necho's sister and successor, regent for his son Psammetichus II. It was an archer of Necho's that shot Josiah, the fifth to last king of Israel, twenty-two years before the destruction of Jerusalem.

Consider what Grimal has done: he gets the overall length of about 900 years for the six dynasties right, and then he gets their division at about 400 and 500 years right, and then he gets the division of the ruling house at the death of Cheops right. And then within that time he names seven names already known to biblical and classical history, placing them pretty much where they belong. For instance, he starts Djoser about 500 years before the end of Nitocris. That is correct. King David in 1089 BC began to reign that long before the end of Nitocris. The odds that all this is nothing more than coincidence are so small that I think it is safe to assume that Israel sprawled, as the first six dynasties, the length and breadth of the Nile Valley and built the pyramids while it was at it. Especially since the next thing Grimal does is win the same sort of lottery again. When he has nailed down the first six dynasties in such a way that they are unmistakable, there is no reason to expect him to go wrong after that. And he doesn't. In terms of relative chronology, he nails down the dynasties that followed on the Kingdom of Israel, the dynasties of the successor empires of Babylon, Persia, Macedon and Rome. In what follows, I use Grimal's own dynastic lengths.

Dynasties 7 and 8, running together says he, occupy 40 years. That is from 589 BC, the end of Nitocris, to 549 BC. This is the era of Babylon to the year when Cyrus was first recognized as King of the Persians, the year he proclaimed liberty to the captives of Babylon. Josephus says this was fifty years after the destruction of Jerusalem. That's right, that destruction being in 600 BC.

Dynasties 9, 10 and 11 then run 120 years to 429 BC. That is the Persian era to the accession of Arsames, the greatest Persian satrap of them all. The Persian kings, to borrow a phrase, had some credit with him.

The 11th Dynasty solely that of Arsames now, then runs 49 years to 380 BC. It was then that Egypt revolted against the Persians.

The 12th Dynasty, running 206 years, goes from 380 to 174 BC and here the Egyptologists discover something new. They say that the rites of this dynasty are indistinguishable from those of the Macedonians in Egypt. That's because this dynasty is the Macedonians in Egypt. The new thing is that they were already in power there well before Alexander. And well they should be, come to think of it. Herodotus, writing in the time of Arsames, said that Psammetichus, Nitocris' father, hedged his claim on the throne with Greek soldiers in brass armor. That was in the 7th century. Come the 4th century, the Greeks, or Macedonians, had taken over as early as 380 BC, twenty-four years before Alexander was born. No wonder the Egyptians claimed him as one of their own, the son of Nectanebo II.

The 12 Dynasty ends with a queen, the daughter, sister, wife and mother of kings as Grimal says quoting an Egyptian text. That will be Cleopatra I who in 174 BC was all that: daughter of the Seleucid Antiochus the Great, sister of Antiochus the Mad, wife of Ptolemy Epiphanes and mother of his son. And just why this dynasty ends with her then is obvious – it was her brother, reigning already over Mesopotamia and Syria that extended his claim to Egypt as well and, to enforce it, invaded the country in 170 BC. It was in 168 BC that the Roman general drew a line in the sand and ran him out. That line is where the saying 'the line in the sand' comes from.

You might say that all Antiochus the Mad meant to do was force the Jews into the Greek era and make them participate in the Olympics. They wouldn't have anything of it. They rebelled and there is the start of the Maccabees in 168 BC. These people, standing on their descent from the royal family of the 5th Dynasty and on their alliance with Rome that meant to destroy Seleucid control of the Near East, reduced Egypt to the chaos of civil war. Which is why Dynasties 13 and 14 are chaotic, a jumbled pile of names that the Egyptologists don't sort out or make heads or tails of. But at least Grimal's dynastic lengths continue to make sense.

Dynasties 13 and 14 first ran for 111 years from 174 to 63 BC which is where Dynasties 15 and 16 start. From that year, 63 BC when the 13th Dynasty was considerably diminished says Grimal, the four dynasties 13, 14, 15 and 16, ran 26 years to 37 BC when the 17th Dynasty started. Then 13 years later, in 24 BC, the 13th Dynasty ended and two years later so did the 14th Dynasty. In 33 AD the 17th Dynasty ended and by 59 AD so had the 15th and 16th Dynasties.

All these dates are according to Grimal's own relative chronology. All I have done, after imposing the constraint of biblical limitations which end Nitocris in 589 rather than 2200 BC, is translate his dates straight on to the real time scale according to his own dynastic intervals. With startling results as anyone familiar with classical history can see.

It was Pompey, under orders from the Senate to reduce the Mediterranean pirates rampant since the fall of Carthage, who in 63 BC took Jerusalem from the Maccabees. That diminished the 13th Dynasty as Grimal says. It was Herod, already made King of the Jews in 40 BC by Octavian and Anthony, who took the same city in 37 BC. That started the 17th Dynasty. And 24 BC, the end of the 13th Dynasty, is when Herod executed his own father-in-law, the last Maccabean king. I'd guess that 22 BC and the end of the 14th Dynasty is when Augustus, on his sickbed and fearful of dying, gave his seal to Agrippa.

Tiberias around 33 AD recognized Caligula as his most likely successor which ended any further hopes the 17th Dynasty, the dynasty of Herod, might have in Egypt. The first ruler of this dynasty is Rahotep. The 'p' is superfluous and 'h' and 'r' are switched around so the name is Harot or Herod.

The 15th and 16th Dynasties meanwhile, running from 63 BC to anywhere near the reign of Nero ending in 68 AD, can only be Rome's rulers from Pompey to Nero, the last of the Julio Claudians. The Egyptologists take those dynasties to be the Hyksos mentioned by Manetho. That would make him a prophet since he died around 270 BC. In a following chapter I will show who he meant.

Now, consider what Grimal has done after getting the critical details of the first six dynasties right. It doesn't matter that his absolute chronology is off by 1600 years.

What matters is that his relative chronology is right. He has successfully picked the seven intervals, the seven numbers 40, 120, 49, 206, 111, 26 and 13 that mark the time from the end of Nitocris in 589 BC to the end of the Maccabees in 24 BC. Each of his intervals, transferred to the real time scale, yields a watershed date in classical history. These dates are not just any random things drawn from a hat. Each of them is known to anyone familiar with classical history. Grimal has just won the lottery again.

There is a lottery in Canada that you win if you pick the same six numbers from a range of one to forty-nine as are drawn, and it doesn't matter whether you have them in the order in which they are drawn. All you have to do is have all six. The odds of winning at one throw are put at one in fourteen million.

Grimal has correctly picked seven numbers drawn from a range of up to two hundred and six and, not only that, he has picked them in the order in which they are drawn by classical history running from 589 to 24 BC. What are the odds of that happening by chance? One in billions I should think.

Since the 15th, 16th and 17th Dynasties end with the last of the Julio Claudians, it is obvious what the 18th Dynasty must be – it can only start with Vespasian and his two sons Titus and Domitian, go on with the Antonines, and finish with the pseudo-Antonines, in my estimation with Odenathus in 268 AD. And that is exactly what the 18th Dynasty is that starts with two brothers, Kamose and Ahmose, which are none other than Titus and his brother.

So far, recognizable men and events have been a trickle but with this dynasty they rise to a flood. Some of its mummies display the same wounds of assassination as are mentioned by the Latin authors.

INTRODUCTION

One of the best works on the 18th Dynasty is the first few volumes of Gibbon's *Decline and Fall of the Roman Empire* which were published around the time of the American Revolution before Egyptology got started. The Egyptological story of this dynasty and the story of the Antonines as Gibbon puts it together are both the same story. So much so that one might wonder whether the Egyptologists used Gibbon's work as a crib sheet. All an Egyptologist has to do to be brilliant is follow Gibbons' lead. Subtly of course so as not to give the game away.

The 19th Dynasty with its Ramses II the Great is the house of Constantine the Great who died in 337 AD. They are both the same man. Obviously, Constantine is not the original Ramses since the name was mentioned before he was born. Confusion arises because Constantine had a habit of taking the monuments of others as his own. I will show who the original was.

Ramses III and the 20th Dynasty are Theodosius and his dynasty. They are both the same man. Sure enough, Grimal puts the same number of years between the deaths of Ramses III and Ramses II as there are between the deaths of Theodosius in 395 AD and Constantine in 337 AD. Grimal gives the 20th Dynasty 119 years which from 363 AD, the end of Julian and Constantine's house, reaches to 482 AD which is where Gibbon ends the dynasty of Theodosius.

On the real time scale, in their discussions of the life and times of Theodosius, the Egyptologists tend to bail out here at the earliest opportunity with the excuse that since the Christian emperor destroyed pagan and ancient Egypt they, the Egyptologists, may as well pack up and go home confident in a job well done. They might add a few remarks to carry things along to the invasions of Chosroes the Persian and then Umar the Arab but that is only by the way. But on their fictitious time scale, where Grimal ends the 20th Dynasty in 1069 BC, there's a long way to go before they can abscond. They have to carry on and so they do.

All the dynasties so far are easy to recognize. They fall naturally into place and can be expected. The 21st Dynasty is the first exception to this rule. But then, why shouldn't it be when the Egyptologists themselves, on the real time scale, take exception to anything after Theodosius as though he were the end of ancient Egypt? After all, here we are after the fall of Rome. After that, there are no more Roman emperors who reigned over Egypt. So who knows what this obscure 21st Dynasty might be? Some barbarians to be sure. Only because the Egyptologists make a good case that it follows on the 20th do I take their word for it. Grimal gives it 124 years which runs from 482 to 606 AD.

This 606 AD is the end of the history of ancient Egypt. A few years later, Chosroes the Persian and then Umar the Arab made sure of that, and this is why the last rulers of the 21st Dynasty moved bodies to safety, that of Constantine for instance. They saw the end coming. That being so, what can the Egyptologists mean with Dynasties 22 through 25 that they stick in there before real time Psammetichus and his 26th Dynasty comes along? With the end of the 21st Dynasty, ancient Egypt is over and so the job of the Egyptologist is over because there aren't any more stories to tell. So what is all this extra stuff about?

The answer to this question is that the Egyptologists have hung themselves out to dry by ending the 21st Dynasty, the end of the story, in 945 BC Grimal's date. They have 281 years to go before Psammetichus and safety. They can't just slide everything down their time scale to him because their system of seasonally adjusted dates forbids it. They can't stack on a following dynasty because it would be suddenly recognizable as belonging to the eras of Chosroes and Umar. They can't stay where they are. What to do? The only thing to do is go back. So back they go. How far? Why, just far enough so that when they stack it on they reach Psammetichus and real time for once.

From 606 AD, Grimal goes back to 293 AD, the start of the 22nd Dynasty. Its identity is revealed by a scholar's remark, Oppert's, that every one of its names is straight from the region of Susa in Southwest Persia near the Mesopotamian border. This can mean only one thing – these are the Sassanids who, starting in the time of Heliogabalus dead in 222 AD, came from there to contest Roman control of the Near East. Around 293 AD Rome made a treaty of peace with them and before he died Theodosius, according to Gibbon, asked them to safeguard the welfare of his less than competent son. Seeing the Goths and Huns coming on, Theodosius took his friends where he found them. Grimal gives the 22nd Dynasty 215 years so that it runs from 293 to 508 AD. So these Sassanids didn't just honor their handshake with Theodosius, they protected his dynasty in Egypt through the collapse of Rome.

The Egyptologists call the 19th year of the last Ramesside of the 20th Dynasty the first year of the Renaissance. That translates to 472 AD toward the end of Theodosius' dynasty. Historians do not agree on the year that Rome fell, their dates varying from 470 to 479 AD. If Grimal's relative chronology is right, the first year of the Renaissance, 472 AD, is the year that Rome fell.

Dynasties 23 and 24 are priests running alongside Dynasties 21 and 22. The 25th Dynasty, overlapping the 22nd by seventeen years according to Grimal, runs by his chronology from 491 to 582 AD. I have adjusted this so that it runs for ninety-one years from 480 to 571 AD. The Egyptologists say that its first ruler, Piankhy, hails from the Sudan. I don't think so. The Egyptologists themselves complain that southern Egypt's texts and monuments sometimes make out as though things happened there when in fact they happened somewhere to the north. That's what we have here. The Egyptological tale of Piankhy reads like Gibbon's tale of Clovis the Merovingian King of the Franks. It was the church that converted that barbarian and declared him King of the Romans. It appears that the church meant to continue the history of Egypt by patching him on to the line of collapsed Caesars.

Grimal needed 281 years and so Dynasties 22 and 25, occupying a span of 289 years, are enough and more to reach Psammetichus and then comes Nitocris whom we last saw ending the 6th Dynasty. The Psammetichides, after ending the 6th Dynasty, now appear again as the 26th Dynasty in the arrangement of Egyptology. From there on everything is familiar history and the Egyptologists can trust the rest of us to get everything right after that.

The real time span of ancient Egypt runs from Joshua to Chosroes. Think of that span as a wide trail of debris 2100 years long. What the Egyptologists have done is go along and divide that into two trails of debris, two windrows, one familiar and one unfamiliar. Into one windrow they put everything that is familiar from the Bible and the classics. Into the other they put all the stuff we never heard of or hardly. Like indigenous names known only to the natives of Egypt at the time. And their odd reign lengths. And their hieroglyphics. And their hieratic script. And their Assyrian correspondence. And their pagan and animistic gods. And their barbarous nonsense made even

INTRODUCTION

more nonsensical by the Egyptologists' less than perfect understanding of what they are reading. And so on.

This unfamiliar windrow of stuff from Joshua to Chosroes the Egyptologists then take, lock, stock and barrel and slide it back by 1600 years in their chronological tables so that it ends with Psammetichus in 664 BC. This backslidden half of history, Dynasties 1 through 25, is what Egyptology is.

CHAPTER ONE

THE REAL SOTHIC CYCLE

You have got to wonder why the Egyptologists are 1600 years high. How is that possible! There are two sides to this question: intent and mechanics. The one side, whether or not the founders of Egyptology raked out that windrow and slid it back on purpose, I must leave to someone with better resources than my own. But I can explain something about the mechanics of it. It's pretty simple really and goes quicker than 'boiled asparagus' as Augustus used to say.

The Egyptologists are 1600 years high because that's where they stopped after lowering their dates in jumps of 1461 years each, their Sothic cycle. In the 19th century they started out with dates one, two, even three of these cycles higher than they are now. The new field of Archaeology forced them to move down the time scale by proving that the strata simply was not there in the ground for any such antiquity as they first supposed. And the strata still wasn't there for them but there they stuck, where they are now, because they were so sure beforehand that ancient Egypt must be a lot older than biblical and classical history.

It did not occur to them, or at least to the public, that

THE REAL SOTHIC CYCLE

their dynasties are the same story we know already and all they had to do to get it right was come down one more cycle where everything comes into focus.

In that case, you might wonder, why the 1600 years? Why not 1461 years, the length of their cycle of seasonally adjusted dates? The reason for this is that the real cycle, the one that is actually played out on the time scale by the Egyptian calendar, runs from 1602 to 1606 of our years. So they are out by one Sothic cycle after all. The old authors put this cycle at 1605 Egyptian years of 365 days each with no leap years. This is almost 1604 of our years which is the average but in what follows I'll call it 1605 years just to maintain the traditional number. Let me explain.

First of all, forget the 1461 year business, a figure gotten by dividing 365.25 days by 0.25 days. The Egyptologists pretend that the year is 365.25 days long and that 0.25 days, 6 hours, is the day fraction lost every year by a 365 day calendar without leap years. In fact, the only reason the old authors mentioned 1461 years at all was to provide an oversimplified example by way of explaining what is actually involved.

What is actually involved is that since the year is more like 365.242199 days long, as the old authors knew very well, any one day of the Egyptian calendar year lost 0.242199 days per year and backed around through the seasons to arrive again at the same star fix it started from, the one that had marked the summer solstice, 1508 years and 9 days later. But it wasn't the star fix the Egyptian year was after. It was the summer solstice that governs the rising of the Nile and the first season of the solar year. The solstice marked the rising heat of summer that melted the snows in the watersheds of Lake Victoria that fed the Nile. This solstice was not there at that star fix anymore due to its precession at the rate of one day every 70.638059 years. So the calendar day, to come into conjunction with the Nile flood again, had to chase the solstice back through the star fixed year.

The math here is like the old high school problem of how long it takes a fast car to catch up with a slow one on a round track after they both leave the starting line together. It took the receding Egyptian calendar day almost 1602 years to catch the precessing solstice and then for four years running the day of the calendar and the new star fixed day of the solstice was on the same day. This was the actual Sothic cycle that was actually in play. So naturally the Egyptologists with their seasonally adjusted dates, dates keyed to the Nile flood which in effect keys them to the summer solstice, can only be either right or 1605 years off. They've chosen to be off which is just as revealing as choosing to be on.

The Greeks called this cycle the apocatastasis of the Egyptian year. Theon of Alexandria, a contemporary of Constantine, said that the apocatastasis of the Egyptian year came to an end in the fifth year of Augustus which was 24 BC. The historians say that the term means what happens when the Egyptian year is let run without any correction of leap years. They assume that Augustus in 24 BC enforced the Julian year with its leap years. He did not. People kept on using the old calendars and the apocatastasis kept on running. Otherwise Censorinus would not have said that a cycle came to an end around 139 AD. Apocatastasis, translated from the Greek, means what happens when something evolves through stages to arrive at equilibrium, a stasis. That's what a cycle is. The annotation, the margin note, on Theon's manuscript reads 'Since Menophres and until the end of the era of Augustus, or

THE REAL SOTHIC CYCLE

the beginning of the era of Diocletian, it was 1605 years'. There's the authentic cycle right there. And who scribbled that note that the historians never fail to observe was written in 'execrable Greek'? Probably one of Pope Gregory's chronologists. From 24 BC to Gregory's calendar in 1582 AD it is 1605 years. Test the ink. It should be consistent with the 16th century AD.

The Egyptologists say that the Sothic cycle is not referred to in the old Egyptian records. Of course it is. That's what the 'whm mswt' is. This Egyptian term is translated as the repetition of births. That's rather clumsy though at least it hints at something cyclical. I'd translate it to mean the end, or beginning of a Sothic cycle where Sothic, after the goddess Sothis, is understood to refer to the summer solstice. The Egyptians represented the solstices with two sky goddesses, each the opposite of the other. Sothis stood for the summer solstice and the onset of the Nile flood. A cycle can be observed to start or end with the summer solstice of any year at all. And so there's nothing wrong with Gregory's chronologists starting theirs in 24 BC and ending it 1605 years later in their time. The only thing that makes a cycle special is when the day coinciding with the solstice happens to be Thoth 1, the first day of the calendar, and all it takes to make some cycle noteworthy is for it to occur in the historical record as observed by somebody. Pope Gregory could say that he was the whm mswt whether he had any interest in the Nile flood or not.

Before Gregory the next one on record to make the claim is Diocletian starting his era circa 284 AD. Sety, of the 19th Dynasty, said he was the whm mswt. Sety is Diocletian.

Before Diocletian it should have been Antoninus Pius or Marcus Aurelius circa 139 AD who would have claimed the whm mswt but the Egyptological record is oddly silent here. Thutmose III is Marcus Aurelius but I haven't read anywhere that he claims the cycle. It seems we have to take Censorinus' word for it that a cycle ended then.

The next previous cycle on record is that of Achoris in 380 BC. He said he was the whm mswt. Meanwhile Grimal starts the 12th Dynasty circa 1991 BC with Amenmesses I who said he was the whm mswt. Since this dynasty is the Macedonians starting in 380 BC, it follows that Achoris and Amenmesses, separated by about 1605 years in Grimal's chronology, are the same man.

So here we have four historical whm mswt's, real Sothic cycles, three of which, Gregory's, Diocletian's and Marcus', each hark back to a time 1605 years before, a time falling in some dynasty or other. The fourth instance, Achoris', is the exception to this rule since 1605 years before him would start his cycle, on the real time scale, in pre-dynastic Egypt half a millennium before the 1st Dynasty, so we can discount finding any record of that. Perhaps he meant to start a cycle, not end one. I've already found the start of Gregory's cycle, so that leaves two to track down, the ones ending circa 139 and 284 AD.

Historians are unsure about the year Censorinus meant as ending a cycle. Their estimates vary from 139 AD to three years later. I find 141 AD works out the best because, in the Julian calendar, 1605 Egyptian years back from the summer solstice of that year starts the cycle with the solstice and Thoth 1 both on the same day, the 18th of July in 1464 BC early in the 1st Dynasty on the real time scale. This is assuming that Thoth 1 coincided in 312 BC with Deos 1, the 7th of October, the beginning of the Seleucid era, the Greek Deos being the same as Thoth the God of Time. That's by the older 360 day Egyptian calendar. In the 15th century BC they did not yet use the 365 day calendar. From the 18th of July in 1464 BC to the 7th of October in 312 BC it is a whole number of 360 day years so that this interval begins and ends with Thoth 1. Furthermore, it appears this 18th of July marked the heliacal rise of Sirius since Grimal says this usually, but not always, happened on the 19th of July in the Julian calendar.

So here we have all the criteria associated with the beginning or end of a Sothic cycle, all falling on the same day: Thoth 1, the heliacal rise of Sirius, the summer solstice and the rising of the Nile, and so, the beginning of the first season of the solar year and of the calendar. Such an extraordinary conjunction of events can hardly have gone unnoticed in the old Egyptian record so let's see if we can find it. It should be there since Censorinus mentioned it.

Since the Egyptologists are 1605 years high, they can be expected to put the event circa 3068 BC and that is exactly what Grimal does. He spends a whole page discussing the tablet of the 1st Dynasty's Djer which he says puts the goddess Sothis and the heliacal rise of Sirius and Thoth 1 and the Nile flood and the 1st season of the year all on the same day, which shows they understood the solar year very well. While he doubts that they employed a 365 day calendar that early (of course not.) he doesn't doubt his late 4th millennium date. Meanwhile of course, due to precession of the solstices, the observations of Djer can only be true in all recorded history for the four years running starting with the 18th of July in 1464 BC. That tablet cannot possibly come from circa 3068 BC because the solstice then was 23 days after the heliacal rise of Sirius, the rise of that star with the sun in the morning.

Since the cycle of Djer ending in 141 AD is the archetype, the cycle ending circa 284 AD can only be imperfect with the heliacal rise of Sirius two days after the solstice. So my interest in tracking down the beginning of this cycle is only to show that, sure enough, Menophres shows up in Egyptology 1605 years earlier than he should.

The Egyptologists say that Menophres is Ramses I starting the 19th Dynasty and they start him 1605 years before 284 AD which is 1321 BC. They give him a reign of one year so that his successor Sety and his whm mswt beginto reign 1604 years before himself, Diocletian. And that is exactly right if you're going to be off by one cycle because 1605 Egyptian years are almost 1604 of our years.

To find Menophres in their chronological tables we have to go back another cycle to their 2926 BC where Grimal ends the 1st Dynasty. Naturally, we can't expect the name Menophres to be emblazoned there because then the Egyptologists would have some trouble supporting their anachronism. The name is Benothres, listed by Africanus as third in the 2nd Dynasty. Either the annotator of Theon's manuscript was scribbling away by dictation – Benothres sounds like Menophres when mumbled – or here we know what they mean by execrable Greek. The Greek 'B' laid on its back looks like 'M', and 'th' is a circle with a horizontal line through it which laid on its back looks like 'ph' which is a circle with a vertical line through it. Whether this is cryptography or just sloppy writing, it appears that Menophres is Benothres and the Egyptologists themselves prove that they are a cycle high. But, as we shall see in Chapter Three, Africanus has the order of the names wrong. Benothres should be fourth in the 1st Dynasty.

CHAPTER TWO

THE EXODUS

IN THE SPRING OF 1519 BC, four hundred and thirty years to the day after Abraham started his travels, the children of Israel set out to leave Misraim in Mesopotamia. That was after about two hundred years in that country, the last century of which was spent at hard labor under cruel treatment. They started from Khuzen or Khuzestan, the biblical Goshen which had been given them to settle by the King, the friend of Joseph. This was cattlemen's country and while there, they could guard the southern approaches to Misraim from raids by the fierce pastoral tribes inhabiting the Zagros Mountains and the uplands of Persia.

At first they went north along the Fertile Crescent, the Way of the Philistines who had entered the country from the Persian Gulf long before. But Moses, in order to avoid a pitched battle with the cruel King, turned about and went south heading for the east shore of the sea of reeds where he knew of an east-west ridge of ground that was barely under water. If he could just get his people along that ridge he could avoid the barriers presented by the Tigris and Euphrates rivers and they could slip away westwards into the deserts and escape that way. I'd guess that this ridge was a sort of dam that kept the two rivers from rushing off into the Gulf and created the huge reservoir of the reed sea, the Hawr al Hammar, to the north and to the south was the Great Canal, now the Shatt al Arab that conducted the overflow to the Gulf. They were told to 'camp at Pi ha Kharith between Migdol and the sea'. Gedol means great so I take Migdol to mean greater. While the reed sea was big, the Persian Gulf was greater. Kharith seems to mean a furrow or a ditch and since a furrow is a ridge of humped earth running alongside a ditch that the earth was ploughed up out of, I take Kharith to refer to the ridge. Pi means the entrance to or the mouth of something. So the passage can be translated as 'camp at the entrance to the land bridge between the greater sea and the sea of reeds'. This Pi ha Kharith would have been at the east end of the land bridge and, remarkably, the place is still there. On my atlas map it is called Al Haritha which is the Arabic form of the Hebrew Ha Kharith. The place is at the southeast edge of the reed sea, pretty much where I expected it to be though I certainly had no expectation of finding it still there on the map.

So there they were camped when the cruel King and his horsemen and chariots caught up with them. He had waited for Moses in the north. On discovering he had been tricked, he left his army to march on as fast as possible and rushed south with his horsemen to find Israel, as he gleefully said, 'entangled in the wilderness '. Moses could not move north because of the approaching army; any escape east was blocked by massed chariots; to the south lay the shores of the Gulf; to the west stretched the sea of reeds. What the King did not realize was that Moses was not trapped at all. He was only waiting for the wind to come up and dry off the ridge. And so they waited, the King waiting for his army to catch up. The wind got there first. Ponderous masses of air slid down the west slopes of the Zagros and howled across the plains and the sea of reeds. All night long it blew and by first light the way west was dry enough to walk on. And so they crossed, their rear secured by the rearguard on that narrow strip of land and the deep water on either side was a 'wall to them' securing their flanks. They got across and just then the wind stopped. The water flowed back to cover the ridge and bog down the chariots and sweep them off one side or the other. And so Ereshu II of Akkad, the cruel King, was beaten by his old enemy Sargon I of Akkad whom we know as Moses.

Pi ha Kharith was 'opposite Baal Zephon' which means 'opposite the unirrigated north country', the north wilderness, or the north desert. And there it is on my atlas map. Across the reed sea from Al Haritha, due west, stretches the Badiyah ash Shamiya which means the North Desert. The Hebrew Baal Zephon is the Arabic Badiyah ash Shamiya. After crossing the reed sea, this north desert country was the first place Moses headed for but here I lose him.

Up to this point, the movements of Israel have been easy to track. There is no doubt in my mind that I have the locations correct so far. But as soon as they get to the North Desert, I lose track for no more reason I think than that the maps available to me simply are not detailed enough. But at least two historical records allow us to catch up to them at the end of their forty year trek.

First, some old Arab historians say that a great army of people were uprooted by disaster and moved through Arabia following a cloud before them to invade and conquer the Nile Valley. That will be Israel. At first there was a cloud pointing the way, which I assume came from the active volcano where Moses carved the tablets, and then there was the cloud over the tabernacle which they followed when it moved and camped when it stood still.

And then there are modern Egyptologists who bring what I assume to be that same army of people, at their inflated date of circa 3100 BC of course, across the Red Sea into Upper Egypt from whence they conquer the country under their standard of the hawk or eagle. Upper Egypt is anything south of the Delta and it isn't clear to me exactly what they mean by the Red Sea. Is it the west arm that defines the west border of the Sinai or is it the main body of water? I've yet to see an Egyptologist mention a hastily constructed navy of watercraft of some sort or other. And why should they so long as they stick to the evidence? According to the Bible, Israel under Joshua crossed a body of water on foot to get to the Promised Land after the priests and the ark dried up the waterbed in the midst of which the twelve tribes playfully left a ring of twelve monoliths. This is a thing of biblical proportions. I suspect that ring of stones is still there, or was for a long time. Some old maps of Egypt show a ring of monoliths to the west of where the Suez Canal later came to be. Maybe they marked the spot. Then Joshua would have put his headquarters in the south out of easy reach of the powerful northern cities. The Egyptologists' army following the standard of the eagle was Israel following the standard of Jacob whose name, among other things, means an eagle.

CHAPTER THREE

DYNASTIES 1 AND 2 ARE THE JUDGES

IN THE TENTH YEAR OF JOSEPH'S RULE OVER MISRAIM IN MESOPOTAMIA, in the third year of the famine, in the spring of 1726 BC, Jacob and his sons and their houses moved there where, being herdsmen, they were given what is now Ghuzistan to settle. Joseph was known to these Mesopotamians as the divine Mesannapada, the name appearing in the cuneiform of the Sumerian King List as the first ruler of the First Dynasty of Ur once this List is placed properly on the real time scale. I wonder if the 's' and 'n' of this name haven't been switched around, if it shouldn't be written more recognizably as Menassahpada, Menassah being one of his sons. From 1726 BC to the Exodus in 1519 BC it is 207 years.

Meanwhile, historians say that the First Dynasty of Egypt was preceded by a 200 year interval that is set apart from all that had gone before by the appearance of Mesopotamian style artifacts, cylinder seals for instance. Evidently, this interval is the time of Israel in Mesopotamia and naturally, starting with Joseph, they would have maintained contacts with the place which they believed was theirs by divine right.

And after those 200 years, say the Egyptologists, the 1st Dynasty burst on the scene in full flower already. No slow evolution of culture here. As soon as they started, they were already fully developed. And not only did they do things Mesopotamian style, the recessed facades and alternate buttresses of walls for instance (an architectural necessity when you're working with sun dried brick), they did it with a workmanship superior to the manufactures found in Mesopotamia. W.B. Emery, in his 1961 *Archaic Egypt*, says this people of the 1st Dynasty were neither indigenes, natives of the country, nor Mesopotamians. They were a third party. But who they were and where they came from except from the east he says he doesn't know.

Emery is right. They weren't indigenes because they were the invaders flying the flag of the eagle that crossed at the ring of the monoliths. And they weren't Mesopotamians either. They were Israel coming from 200 years in Mesopotamia. Of course they did things better than the Mesopotamians did because they, starting with Joseph, were the ones who invented and developed the arts and technology of Mesopotamia and now they were in the land promised them; naturally they made a better job of it.

And when Joshua conquered the country, he did not make a total conquest. He left strong settlements of the natives here and there. His idea, he said, was that Israel should not go soft and forget the arts of war. It was a good thing, he said, that Israel should be obliged to defend itself now and then. This odd generosity of his, and of his successor judges, is duly noted by the Egyptologists who observe that the first two dynasties, the time of the judges, lived side by side in some tension with the indigenes of the country. This generosity came to an end with Djoser of the 3rd Dynasty who started the era of kings and empire. That will be David who finally had enough of this cat and mouse business. After the deaths in battle against the Philistines of the two men he most admired, Saul the Mad and Jonathan, David set out to crush all opposition and that is what he did.

In the fortieth year of the Exodus Moses commanded that they write 'their goings out according to their journeys by the commandment of the Lord'. The Hebrew word that is translated 'goings out' means borders, but borders of a special kind – they demarcated any one region with two lines, two borders, only. The ends of the lines 'went out' which is to say that they were not fixed. They retreated or advanced according to the fortunes of the holder. When cultivatable or habitable lands were extended and when opposition from foreign claims was quashed, the lines extended. Otherwise, the ends of the border lines stayed where they were or retreated. In other words, a region had two borders that were fixed, say its north and south borders, and two that were not fixed, its east and west borders. The land claim was open ended. This type of demarcation is particularly suited to a valley of rich bottom land, the valley being marked off with transverse borders, the ends of which run wild up into mountains or off into the desert.

So now we know how to understand those sentences in the 33rd chapter of the Book of Numbers which read 'These are the journeys of the children of Israel which went forth out of the land of Misraim with their armies… And Moses wrote their goings out according to their journeys… and these are their journeys according to their goings out…'

and there follows the list of the 42 journeys or camps from the first one in Misraim where they set out to the last one forty years later on the border of the Promised Land. In other words, 'These are the journeys or camps... And Moses wrote their borders according to these camps... and these are their camps according to those borders'. So Moses commanded that Israel shall divide the Promised Land into 42 provinces, a province for a camp, each province a memorial of the camp it stood for. And, more remarkably, the authors of the Masoretic version of the Old Testament come right out and say that they did not pore over the topography of the Arabian deserts to track down the 42 camps there. As they say, 'these are their camps according to those borders'. That is, they took the easy way out and listed the camps simply by referring to the 42 provinces of the land that Israel conquered and occupied. Incidentally, these Masorite authors were Hebrews living in exile after the fall of Jerusalem. Their land of exile was Babylonia. The historians profess not to know why these authors and their Hebrew version were called Masoretic and suppose that the term refers to these authors' addition of vowel points, punctuation, and so on, to earlier texts. In fact, there is nothing complicated or obscure here. The version is called Masoretic after its country of origin, Musri in Mesopotamia, Misraim, the same way that the version written in Syria is called Syriac.

Besides the 42 minor divisions, the provinces according to the camps as ordained by Moses, the Promised Land was divided into two major parts which I find in the Book of Joshua chapters 15 through 18 which says that in the sixth year of the conquest the land was divided between the house of Joseph in the north and the house of Judah in the south. This primary division of the land continued in effect providing the basis centuries later for Jeroboam, whom Solomon had put over the house of Joseph, to secede taking the north half with him. It was only some time after this division of the land into two major parts that Joshua divided the land by lot to the unawarded seven tribes and their lots were awarded within the lands of Joseph in the north and Judah in the south. This was done after twenty-one men, three from each of the seven tribes with pending claims, divided the whole land in 'seven parts' which was in sevens, three sevens in the north and three sevens in the south for 21 and 21 totaling 42. It was these surveyors who carried out the command of Moses that the land be divided according to the 42 camps.

Meanwhile, ancient Egypt since the earliest dynasties was divided into 42 provinces or nomes as the Greeks called them. According to the 1984 Time-Life Atlas of Ancient Egypt, these nomes had fixed north and south borders but were open ended on the east and west where their 'goings out' ran up into the mountains bordering the Nile Valley or out into the desert. With the 5th Dynasty, says the Atlas, these nomes were divided to put 22 in the south, running from the 1st at Aswan to the 22nd at Memphis, and 20 in the north running from the 1st at Memphis and on around through the Delta. This division at 22 and 20 is not the more perfect 21 and 21 but so much the better because at the secession of the north, the 4th Dynasty, the tribe of Benjamin occupying its south border cast in its lot with the south, the throne of Judah, which is the 5th Dynasty. So here we have not only the biblical number of provinces but also their division into north and south as the Bible divides them.

Long odds might make all this a coincidence but those odds approach zero when I observe that four camps were unique for plague, death and disaster, the camps numbering 13, 20, 36 and 40, while at the same time four nomes are unique in having each in its ensign the sign of what appear to be three censers standing in a row and counting the nomes 1 through 42 consecutively from the south, these four nomes are numbered like the camps, 13, 20, 36 and 40. While each of these four has also a second glyph distinguishing it from the other three, they all four share the sign of the censers implying something solemn which I take to hark back to what happened at the corresponding camps.

Furthermore, the ensign of the 39th nome suddenly and uniquely introduces the glyph for land or country. Nome 40 has, besides the sign of the censers the glyph of the infant King. The ensign of nome 41 also has the infant King. And the ensign of nome 42 has the hawk of Horus with a crown of two feathers resting on a couch. These last four ensigns are a group implying landed sovereignty and these correspond well with the last four camps when Israel led by Moses defeated the two Syrian Kings Sihon and Og (the two feathers in the hawks crown) and occupied their lands as the first conquered territories. And the people rested in the 42nd camp just before invading the Nile Valley which same rest appears on the ensign as the hawk resting on the couch.

According to the Atlas, 42 was not just the number of nomes. It had also a symbolic value. There were 42 Judges of the Dead and Clement of Alexandria in the 2nd century AD said that the Egyptians had 42 sacred books. Of course the number 42 had a symbolic value – each nome was symbolized by a camp and the 42 camps were taken to symbolize trials or stations of life.

The time of the judges, which is the time of the first

two dynasties, is given by the long count of Solomon who put 480 years from the Exodus through his fourth year of sole rule. So, subtracting his four years and David's forty, that is 436 biblical years of 360 day years, which are almost 430 of our years for the time of the judges from Moses at the Exodus to the end of Saul. King Saul was counted as a judge because Judge Samuel, who made him King, changed his mind in favor of David. Meanwhile, Grimal gives the first two dynasties, the judges, 450 years. I think he can be excused from a twenty year error here. This interval of 430 years was begun by Narmer, a name the Egyptologists read because he signed his name with a fish, 'Nar', and a wedge shaped object they take to be a chisel, 'Mer'. But before Narmer some old Egyptian records name Menes, a person for whom the Egyptologists find no evidence at all. However, I can guess who this is because, as Grimal says, his name is written twice, once with the human determinative and again with the divine determinative. What we have here is the divine Menesapada, or, as the eastern cuneiform seems to have it, the divine Mesannapada. Joseph the Divine or the Diviner, I'm not sure which. So the Egyptians, sensibly enough, started that 200 year preamble to the First Dynasty with Joseph. But here, I'm only guessing. With Narmer however we don't have to guess. His identity is revealed by unmistakable pictograms, pictures. Let's take a look at some mace heads and votive palettes.

    It is a sorry fact that for some crucial evidence on the beginning of the 1st Dynasty we are reduced to knickknacks, dress parade mace heads that never saw war and fancy pigment mortars, palettes, that were never used. These were grave goods, votive offerings deposited in graves. But at least these grave goods had pictures carved on them that are most revealing indeed, pictures carved in stone that has not faded. And furthermore, they seem to date from the era of the scenes depicted or not long after.

There is the Hunters' Palette which Grimal describes as showing, on one side, a hunt of the sort Assyrians and Persians were later to be famous for – beaters sweeping the countryside to drive wild game into traps. Now we know one way that Israel survived its forty years in the wilderness. On the other side, says Grimal, are men organized military fashion with bows, spears, axes, throw sticks (the first boomerangs), and maces under the ensign of the hawk and the ensign with the hieroglyphic sign that would come to stand for the direction of east. The hawk ensign stands for Israel and the east ensign stands for Judah, the tribe that led the march. Moses ordered that Israel should camp in four quarters, three tribes to a quarter, with the tabernacle and the ark in the center. If you flew over the camp it would look like a Celtic cross with the central area of the tabernacle and four avenues running out to define the four quarters, each quarter in one of the four directions. The east quarter was under the ensign of Judah and Moses ordered that as they camped, east, south, west and north so should they march with the east ensign in the lead. And that is just how the Hunters' Palette shows it.

Furthermore, says Grimal, this side of the Palette shows a 'holy shrine' and a bull with two heads. This shrine, which we can assume to be a depiction of the ark itself covered en marche to protect its jewelry from blowing desert sands, and this two headed bull, pretty well fix the provenance of this Palette to the Exodus or soon after when the people's memory of the ordeal was still fresh. In sheer historical terms, I find the two headed bull almost as interesting as the ark itself because it was Jereboam, the secessionist, who said 'Behold thy gods O Israel who brought thee up out of Misraim'. And so he fashioned what is translated in our Bibles as two 'golden calves' which he placed, for the people's convenience, in two different places. His 'gods' and the Palette's two heads of the bull are Moses and Aaron. Meanwhile, Grimal says that the sovereignty of the land and royalty was interchangeably symbolized by the bull and the lion. So what, we might wonder, did Jereboam's 'golden calf' look like? Did it feature the body of a bull with the head of a man or was the body that of a lion? You can see where I'm going with this. Cheops is Solomon and Chephren, his successor, is Jereboam and it was Chephren who made the Sphinx that has the body of a lion with the head of a man. There's your 'golden calf', the main one.

And there is the Battlefield Palette where the same two ensigns of the hawk, Israel, and the east, Judah, take the enemy prisoner, the enemy being long haired, bearded and wearing the penis-sheath. So now we know what Israel was up against – dirty savages sporting penis-sheaths. We can take it for granted that Israel, circumcised and modestly clothed viewed its enemy with all the disdain and superiority of the 19th century Englishman beholding the savages of darkest Africa. And sure enough, they, Israel and the English, were right because the savages, once beaten, couldn't wait to take on the customs and manners of their betters. Israel was the first to bring the Near East, kicking and screaming, into the modern age. And since the oceans, contrary to modern historians, were a highway rather than an obstacle, it wasn't long until the whole world, east to China and the South Seas and west to the Americas became aware that a new step had been taken in the evolution of mankind. From the time of Solomon and his naval expeditions with Tyre, that's Greater Tyre which is not the same as that miserable little port on the Lebanese coast, the higher cultures of the Americas take their rise.

And there is the Bull Palette showing the prisoners of what Grimal calls 'five federated kingdoms'. These are what the Bible calls the five allied Kings of Midian. On the other side is the picture of two castled towns with, as Grimal says, the names of two conquered peoples written in pictograms. Those two names should read Sihon and Og, the two kings that Moses and Joshua conquered along with the five kings.

And then there is the Narmer Palette where the evidence gets so specific that there is no doubt what we are looking at. The monogram has the Mesopotamian façade motif used by his successors but unlike them it does not have the usual hawk perched on top. Instead, he has the fish and a wedge shaped object. This signs his name which linguists read as Nar for fish and Mer for chisel. However, I see that this is not just any old fish. It is a specific type of fish, a flat fish with both eyes together plainly portrayed on top its head and it has the top fin and whiskered mouth of the flatfish. It isn't pretty, but it does convey just the name I would expect as the forerunner of the 1st Dynasty. This fish is a plaice or a flounder and its name in Arabic is the Samak Musa, the Moses fish. I suppose when the princess of Misraim pulled the infant Moses from the Euphrates, she called him her little flounder and the name stuck. The Bible says that his name Musa is from the Misraim language meaning one pulled out from the river which is what one does with a fish.

Narmer is shown victorious in battle and behind him appears a young man with a pair of sandals on his left arm and a water pitcher in his right hand. This is Narmer's aide who accompanied him which makes him Joshua the aide and successor of Moses. His name is signed by a jar with a star above it. Four standards in front of Narmer represent the standards of the four quarters of the camp of Israel. The east side carried the standard of Judah; the south side Reuben; the west side Ephraim; the north side Dan. Three tribes to a side. And as they encamped, so they marched, starting with Judah and his quarter and ending with Dan on the rearguard.

Narmer, his aide and a third figure view two rows of five decapitated bodies in each row. These I would guess to be the five Kings of Midian and their five army commanders. This would make the figure in front of Narmer to be Phinehas as it says in chapter 31 of Numbers, Moses sent the army against Midian with '...Phinehas the son of Eleazar the priest, to the war, with the holy instruments, and the trumpets to blow in his hand'. This third figure carries over his left shoulder two curved horns! These look to be about four feet long with dust caps over the bell mouths. Only a priest was allowed to blow these one-piece silver horns. At the bottom of the picture is a man with the headgear of a priest slain before an altar. As soon as chapter 31 names the five executed Kings of Midian, it adds that the Mesopotamian priest '...Balaam also, the son of Beor, they slew with a sword'. This proximity of the Kings of Midian to the Mesopotamian Balaam implies that this Midian is Mitanni on the upper Euphrates not down in Arabia somewhere. The other side of the Palette shows Narmer victorious over two men that can only be Sihon and Og.

The dress parade Narmer mace head shows him with his court facing the four standards while three men reverentially approach him surrounded by what Emery says is an account of the spoils of war: so many thousand captives, oxen, goats and in a hand-carried contraption was a woman that probably represents the women captives that were virgins. Chapter 31 of Numbers gives the count of captives and livestock taken from Midian: 675,000 sheep; 72,000 cattle; 61,000 asses; and 32,000 virgins. But the mace head, according to Emery, shows different numbers: 120,000 captives; 400,000 oxen, and 1,422,000 goats.

I'd guess this mace head count is from the lands of Sihon and Og and the three men represent the three tribes of Reuben, Gad and half Manasseh coming to ask Moses as they did, for these lands for their home. 'We will build cattle and sheep pens for our stock and then go help our brothers' they said. And, sure enough, the mace head pictures cattle pens, corrals, which the Egyptologists mention. These lands provide the original historical basis for the false tradition of Palestine.

According to the Bible, the two and a half tribes almost started a civil war when they built in their lands of Palestine a copy of the authentic holy place in the Promised Land. When the rest of Israel heard of this copy, they and Joshua prepared for war on their own kin who appeared to set themselves up as rivals. Only the earnest and truthful explanation offered by a delegation from the two and a half tribes prevented their extinction. They explained that their copy was only a memorial, a proof, of their relation to the rest of Israel so that in the future, when memory of the past faded, their descendants would only have to mention this copy to prove their bona fides and gain admission to the rites and privileges of their brothers the Chosen People. Joshua, on hearing this argument was persuaded and called off the war. And so the copy was built that eventually led to the false tradition of Palestine.

So far we have the name Menes whom I take to be Joseph and then some lists write the word 'king' twice which I

take to mean various kings that go unnamed until Narmer. In other words, that two hundred year preamble to the 1st Dynasty is accounted for by Joseph and several unnamed kings, and then came Narmer. After him, the Egyptologists enter Horaha, the Fighting Hawk, which can only be Joshua through the five years of the conquest and then they enter Djer which they translate as the Scorpion. This Djer is also Joshua. So far as I can see, he changed his name once the conquest was achieved. He ruled for thirty seven years, the first five as Fighting Hawk, then thirty two as Scorpion.

Consider the mace head of the Scorpion King Djer. His name is signed by what appears to be a pot with appendages added so the pot resembles a scorpion. And over this pot turned scorpion is the very same star that appears over the pot of Narmer's aide. This Djer is none other than Narmer's aide come to power. These people, Djer and his people, were Hebrews. And this Hebrew language was cognate, almost the same as, with classical Arabic. In Arabic, jarra is a pot and jarara is a certain type of scorpion. The aide to Narmer and the Scorpion King are the same man, and this man, Joshua, was no more called the Scorpion than he was called the Pot. Both these words are determinatives that modify, add meaning to, the sign of the star. And we don't have to wonder what this star sign stands for; it stands for the star Sirius as we know from the Djer tablet already mentioned. The Egyptian hieroglyphic for a pot has various associated meanings including heat and water. That will be the heat of summer brought on by the summer solstice and the consequent water of the Nile flood. This means that Djer, as early as when he was only aide to Narmer, had observed the coincidence, on the same day, of the heliacal rise of Sirius and the summer solstice.

Those two things occurred on the same day for seventy years, the time it takes for the precessing solstice to move back through one day. But for only four of these years did the first day of the calendar also fall on that day.

The Egyptologists put Horaha, or Fighting Hawk, between Narmer and Djer so this must also be Joshua who then had three names for three stages of his career: the name signed by the star and the pot; the one signed by the fighting hawk which would be him during the five years of the conquest; and the one signed by the star and scorpion for the last thirty two of his years as judge. The Djer mace head shows him at peace with a hoe opening a canal and above him in a row are ensigns but not only four this time. The mace is damaged so that ten ensigns are shown in whole or in part but fragments and space for two more are there also, so that originally, there were twelve ensigns displayed. When referring to times where Israel was on the move or at war, the ceremonial works of art show only the four lead ensigns, but as soon as Israel was at peace, under Joshua as Djer, all twelve ensigns of the twelve tribes are shown. The ensigns have each a dead bird hanging which are said to symbolize the enemy peoples of northern Egypt.

Egyptologists often disagree on the order of the rulers of the first two dynasties and on which names should be included. For instance, some say that Narmer was the first ruler of the 1st Dynasty while others say he was the forerunner and Horaha was first. They are both right. Moses was the first leader and judge over a sovereign Israel but since he died at the border of the Promised Land, it was Joshua who was first leader and judge there.

And there's the lady ruler Meryet Neith who is given anything from third to sixth place on the list. Some say she was a ruler in her own right and others say she was regent for the one named Den. This is the only lady ruler the Egyptologists recognize until Nitocris, and here she is just about where I expect to find her in the 1st Dynasty. She is Judge Deborah, the sixth ruler starting from Moses and she ruled in her own right. Meryet Neith is said to mean the victorious Neith. Deborah was victorious; she planned and won the battle with Jabin and Sisera. Before her was Judge Shamgar who is Benothres, or Menophres. After her was Judge Gideon, whose name means a bold young man, pretty much the same meaning as the name Anedjib, 'the man with the bold heart', which follows Meryet Neith.

    Gideon was succeeded by his son Abimelek, the only father and son pair among the judges. For some reason, Grimal lumps Anedjib with his successor for 45 years. Gideon's 40 and Abimelek's 3 are 43 years.

    The fifteenth judge after Moses was the strongman Samson. Grimal puts Sekhemib, 'the man with the powerful heart', in the fifteenth place. But if he counted Horaha and Djer as the same man as I do, then he would match Sekhemib with Judge Elon. But then at least he would have Per Ibsen, the gentleman Ibsen, in thirteenth place where I find Judge Ibsen.

    Grimal ends the 2nd Dynasty with Khasekhem whose title includes the word 'crowned' for the first time and the Horus hawk of his monogram wears the crown for the first time. Emery says this is the man who, according to Manetho, was five cubits and three palms tall which is about eight feet. So here we have Saul counted as the last judge. He was the first to be recognized as King and he is said in the Book of Samuel to have stood 'head and shoulders' taller than anyone else. Saul, at the end, was counted as a judge because he was dismissed from kingship in favor of David. 'Is Saul among the prophets?', that is, 'among the judges?' the people asked. Yes, he was, according to the Egyptologists.

Of the seventeen judges, the first eight, Joshua to Tola, ruled alone. Then, starting with Jair the ninth judge, there were two or more at a time each with his own jurisdiction. Judges Jair and Eli started at about the same time though I make Eli tenth. And when Eli's forty years ended halfway through Elon's reign, that's when Samson and Samuel began. These two systems of government, where one judge ruled and then more than one, can be described as two dynasties, with eight rulers in the 1st Dynasty and nine in the 2nd. And that is what Africanus has in his copy of Manetho except that the names are not in the right order. He has the first three right; then he jumps to the fifth name; then he has four triplets each of whose three names should be the fourth from the next; then he ends the list with the sixteenth name. Using their true place numbers, he has the names in this order where I've marked off the triplets: 1, 2, 3, 5, / 6, 10, 14, / 7, 11, 15, / 4, 8, 12, / 9, 13, 17, / 16.

Number 4 there, the eleventh number along, is Benothres the eleventh name on Africanus' list. In fact, he was 4th on the list. He decided women could reign, Meryet Neith his successor. It was Shamgar, the 4th judge, who decided women could reign, Deborah his successor. Benothres is Shamgar.

If you write the numbers 1 to 16 in a block of four lines, four numbers to a line, you will see the triplets in the vertical rows. What happened was that the hieroglyphics, the names, were written in a block one way but Manetho read them another. The Egyptologists suspect that Africanus' list is not in order but since the names are Greek form that as a rule are not found archeologically, they've not been able to correct it.

Now that we can go and dig up the goods on the judges and kings of Israel and see what they were actually like and what they actually did, it is inevitable that we should get a shock now and then. I refer you to the well constructed graves with their bodies, numbering up to hundreds of them, which formed a perimeter around mausoleums of 1st Dynasty rulers. Emery says that these are the bodies of the people who were sacrificed, but since he does not mention any wounds I have to wonder whether they simply drank the hemlock. To share in the afterlife of their beloved master of course. I can imagine a sort of Last Supper. What we have here it seems to me is what the later prophets condemned as 'causing your sons and daughters to pass through the fire in the manner of the sons of Hinnom', the sons of the Queen of Heaven. To pass a body through the fire does not mean to reduce it to ashes, it means to mummify it. But to get to that stage, the person has to be dead first. And it is that death, whether by ritual murder or voluntary suicide, that the prophets condemned as outrageous, as something that God never required of his people.

They brought this custom with them from Mesopotamia where Sir Leonard Wooley found the same sort of thing in the royal graves at Ur. In one of these, Wooley found the statue of the ram caught in the thicket and his first thought was of the bible story. This first thought was correct. That grave was contemporary with Joseph who probably put that statue there himself.

CHAPTER FOUR

CHEOPS IS SOLOMON

THE STORY OF DJOSER, heading up the 3rd Dynasty and starting the era of kings and empire, is pretty much how we can expect the Egyptologists to tell the story of David. Djoser completed the unfinished business of unifying the north and the south. That's what David did. He conscripted all people not of Israel in his borders for labor. The Famine Stela set up by a Ptolemy is patterned on an event in the life of Djoser where he learns what he must do to prevent a seven year famine. It was David in the Book of Samuel who learned what he must do to avoid a seven year famine. Djoser in his old age was accompanied by young beautiful women whose job it was to cheer him up and keep him interested in life. It was David who was accompanied in his old age by at least one beauty put there by a busybody staff because he 'got no heat'. This tale is unique in Egyptology and is just as unique in the Bible. Djoser harnessed his domain to a focus on buildings of a design and scale without precedent. That is what David did. Djoser is associated with a man, Imhotep, who was the paragon of wisdom. So is David. Imhotep can only be Solomon.

Of all the wisdom of Imhotep, a keen knowledge of botany and writing proverbs for instance, only one thing seems offhand not to fit Solomon: Imhotep was said to have invented the art of 'building with hewn stone'. But in the Bible it was Hiram, the specialist sent from Tyre by King Hiram who showed David and Solomon the art of stone craft. How then could Solomon have been credited with inventing it? Perhaps all that was meant was the introduction of large scale masonry into the Nile Valley which began with Imhotep. Or, if Solomon actually did invent something, perhaps what we have here is the invention of concrete. So far as I know, neither the Romans nor Greeks claimed the discovery.

In Davidovits 1988 book *The Pyramids: An Enigma Solved*, he points out that Herodotus' Greek should be translated as 'polished stone' not 'hewn stone' and that this term should be understood to mean concrete. After studying the large blocks of the pyramid of Cheops, he finds that these are not hewn stone but are rather a species of concrete. The arrangement of particulates in these blocks are jumbled, as can be expected in concrete, not layered as can be expected in naturally occurring stone. If these blocks were poured rather than hewn, that would explain the mystery of the logistics of building a pyramid as well as joinery found by Petrie to average 1/50th of an inch over 35 square feet.

I like the idea that Solomon invented concrete. The temple after all was said to have been built with no hewing and no sound of a hammer, though this of course is usually taken to mean the blocks were cut elsewhere. Who better than he, the originator of Solomon's seal, to invent the alchemy of masonry? What more useful philosopher's stone could there be than concrete? Alchemy promised that the right mixture of certain commonplace substances could be transformed into something valuable and here it is – concrete.

Among his achievements is something in chapter 10 of I Kings: '... moreover the King made a great throne of ivory and overlaid it with the best gold. The throne had six steps, and the top of the throne was round behind: and there were stays on either side on the place of the seat, and two lions stood beside the stays. And twelve lions stood there on the one side and on the other upon the six steps: there was not the like made in any Kingdom'. This, it seems to me, is a spectacular instance of an original text mutilated by old copyists and then further distorted by bad translation. Are we to understand that there were six steps up to the chair and that the chair actually had armrests? And that its top was round behind, whatever that means, and that lions lolled on the steps to frighten visitors? Why just six steps? Why not twelve? Any two-bit kinglet could have a chair as tawdry as this. I propose to restore this throne to its original biblical proportions, the only kind of proportion that is appropriate when a Bible story is involved.

At least the six steps have survived the copyists. Solomon did build something with six steps only it wasn't a chair. It was a pyramid; the stepped pyramid which has six steps. 'Throne of ivory' is a mistranslation of the Hebrew qsa-sn, the hyphen added by the Masoretes. The hyphen doesn't belong there. The word qsasn which is a form of the cognate Arabic khzn means a keep or storehouse or treasury of some kind. Where the word 'throne' occurs in the quote, that is because of the sn of qsa-sn has been dropped as a sort of abbreviation. But the meaning is not abbreviated. It starts out as a storehouse and it stays that way throughout. This same stepped storehouse is known today as the first pyramid of Egypt, the stepped pyramid of Djoser designed and built by Imhotep. This structure began as the same sort of mausoleum as was built by the first two dynasties, which was a makhzan, or magazine, more or less square. The popular term for a magazine like this in the Arab world is mastaba, a bench. The proper term is makhzan as in a magazine of gunpowder, whether in a fort or in a warship, as it was adopted by the British.

This magazine, which was first intended as Djoser's gravesite, was then extended to the north and west so that it covered most of the pyramid's ground plan while its southeast corner was the southeast corner of the first step of the pyramid. The top surface of this first step, that ran 'round behind' on each of the four sides, was the top of two inclined layered walls leaning in toward the central core, 'the top'. These two outside layers leaned on two more which rose higher to the second step. This second pair in turn leaned on a third pair of inclined walls which rose higher to the third step and so on to the sixth step which was the top of one inclined wall, the innermost, and the outermost face of the central core which will count as a wall, to get twelve walls round behind on the four sides leaning on the top or center. In this way, twelve walls, not lions, 'stood there on the one side and on the other' rising, in their six pairs, to six steps and these 'stays' on the four sides leaned 'on the place of the seat', the central core. According to Edwards in his 1947 book *The Pyramids of Egypt*, the finished structure was 411 feet east and west, 358 north and south and 204 high. It stood in the midst of a one of a kind complex of buildings and the whole was surrounded by a wall 33 feet high that enclosed a space 909 feet wide and 1791 feet long north and south. This wall is the Mesopotamian style series of buttressed recesses,

76 buttresses on the long side if you count two for each mock door. Breaking the flat line of the wall in this way gives the impression that it is rippling in the wind like a great curtain hung on posts. There is something familiar about running a long curtain on posts to make an enclosure twice as long as wide which is what the wall dimensions nearly come to. It was the court of the wayfaring tabernacle that was formed by joining curtains on posts for an enclosure twice as long as wide.

Going from the enclosure wall to the innermost extremity, the tomb chamber under the stepped pyramid, I find there also a near coincidence of proportion. This chamber contains a granite box 'approximately 9 feet 9 inches in length and 5 feet 6 inches both in width and height...' says Edwards. This is the ratio of length to width to height of 5.218:3:3 which is comparable to the 5:3:3 ratio of the ark of the tabernacle. It was unlawful for anyone to use the sacred for secular purposes so I would not expect to find anywhere a sarcophagus with a 5:3:3 ratio in its dimensions.

The historians believe Djoser was laid in that granite box beneath the stepped pyramid. At the same time, the Book of Kings says David was buried in the city of David. If the historians are right, and there's no reason they shouldn't be, it follows that the 'city of David' is the city-like complex of the stepped pyramid of Djoser. The term 'city of David' usually refers to Bethlehem and it would be convenient if the Djoser site marks the vicinity of the authentic Bethlehem, but this does not necessarily follow since there was more than one 'city of David'. Ziklag for example was a 'city of David'. Incidentally, the body of David must have required a large sarcophagus. Saul would not have offered his armor to wear against Goliath unless it fitted. Saul was a big man.

Under the southeast side of the pyramid, spaced along the east wall of the hidden magazine, the mastaba, are eleven shafts going down 108 feet, deeper than the tomb chamber, and then they go west as level galleries to about midline under the magazine. In these were sarcophaguses that are thought to be for the King's family. Eleven is a likely number of David's wives who gave him children. Excluding Saul's daughter who grew to hate him so she would not be represented here, there are six named wives and then the seventh is Bathsheba, the most important wife, and the remaining wives go unnamed. It so happens that, counting from the southeast corner, the seventh gallery is angled to reach to very nearly under the center of the magazine to occupy in that way pride of place. There, with the remains of another sarcophagus presumably for the seventh wife, was found a sarcophagus with the remains of a child. Only once does the death of a child enter the story of David and that is the death of Bathsheba's firstborn son. Solomon was her second born.

After David, his successor descendants were buried in the 'city of David' and this continued until Hezekiah was interred there and then the practice ceased, probably because of the lack of security with the incursions of the Assyrians. The exact number of these successor burials in the precincts is not clear to me because of varying wording for the burial place but it is from ten to thirteen. That is about the number of rooms off the galleries running out from the central tomb chamber. Alternatively, the 'sepulchers of the kings' in the complex might be under the long magazine along the west wall which has not been properly explored due to dangerously unstable rock.

CHAPTER FIVE

DIODORUS SICULUS GETS CHEOPS RIGHT

IN HIS BOOK *THE MOUNTAINS OF PHARAOH*, Cottrell quotes Diodorus to say, 'The largest (pyramid of Cheops) is ... of difficultworkmanship but eternal duration; for in the thousand years said to have elapsed since their construction, which some make more than three thousand four hundred, the stones have not moved from their original position, but the whole remains uninjured'. Diodorus wrote this around the year 20 BC and so his millennium, being of 354 day years, reaches back to circa 989 BC. His authority for this date is the work of official and recognized Greek and Latin historians starting with Theopompus, a contemporary of Philip of Macedon, and with Ephorus, a contemporary of Alexander. These people and their scholarly successors right down to Diodorus had the official duty of laying out the historical context of just how it was that the Greeks came into the possession of Egypt. Diodorus is so confident of his sources that it is with complacency, and even condescension, that he informs us that some make that

DIODORUS SICULUS GETS CHEOPS RIGHT

thousand years out to be 'more than three thousand four hundred'. Little did he know that wildly revisionist twenty-four hundred years extra would be polished down in our modern era to inflation little less crazy, an inflation of 1605 years and become the received wisdom. While Diodorus and his peers used to dismiss the revisionists, now they dismiss him. Today's historians dispose of Diodorus' date for Cheops by saying that he didn't understand Ephorus properly. But of course he understood him properly. Cheops is Solomon and only a fool would put Solomon so far back as the 3rd millennium BC.

Different nations had different names for any one ruler of Egypt. Solomon for instance. His contemporary Hebrews called him Jedidiah, the Chosen of God among other things. His contemporary indigenes called him Imhotep, and Sneferu and Khufu. The Hebrews of the exile, the ones who put the Old Testament together, called him Solomon. The Greeks in Egypt, picking up on Khufu, called him Cheops. And the old Arab historians, whenever they weren't callinghim Suleiman, called him Surid. Surid means the same as Khufu which is, according to the context, the Frightful or the Affrighted, the Scary or the Scared. This name seems to come from Solomon's reputation as a great wizard, a name well deserved since even modern engineers cannot imagine how he built the Great Pyramid. And even if they could imagine it, then they'd have to imagine how he built several others as well, starting with the stepped pyramid of Djoser. The reason modern engineers are confounded by the Great Pyramid is because they assume, on Herodotus' say-so, it was built in twenty years. Davidovits accepts this twenty years and solves the wizardry by showing the twenty ton blocks stacked up over the core are poured concrete. The trouble with this is that it does not account for the fact that the same man built other pyramids as well. The Great Pyramid was only his masterpiece. So let me offer the solution – why should we listen to Herodotus and his twenty years when the builder himself said he finished it in the 61st year of construction? These twenty years of Herodotus is one reason the Arab historians called him the father of lies.

Cottrell quotes the Arab historian Masud to say that Surid inscribed in characters that could be read as Arabic the words, 'I, Surid the King, have built these pyramids and have finished them in 61 years'. That is Solomon talking and with that we don't have to guess where Diodorus' 1000 years goes on the real time scale. Solomon reigned 17 years with his father and then 3 years alone so that he had 60 years left when he began to build in his fourth year of sole rule. Those are biblical years of 360 days each. Since Surid, Solomon, calls this long interval 61 years, he is using the lunar based year of 354 days. It so happens that 60 biblical years is only six days longer than 61 lunar based years. This interval when Solomon did all his building began in the late spring of 1047 BC and ended, with his reign, in early summer of 988 BC. One thousand years after that, years of 354 days which is the year that Diodorus used, ends toward the fall equinox of 19 BC when Diodorus was writing.

So there it is. Diodorus ends Cheops in 988 BC after a 61 year interval of building. It follows that Cheops is Solomon since the reign matches; the interval matches; and the only builder par excellence in Solomon's time was himself.

Masud adds that Surid 'caused the pyramids to be haunted with living spirits' and he describes some of these. For instance, the spirit of the Great Pyramid was in the shape of a boy with large teeth and a sallow countenance.

This tale amounts to Surid signing himself as Solomon. Of all the great kings, only Solomon had the reputation of being the master of magic and sorcery. Egyptology touches on this by reporting that Cheops inquired into the rites of Thoth.

Herodotus describes the logistics of Cheops' building program. I don't know how anyone can read this without getting the impression that it is a garbled version of the logistics of Solomon's building program as laid out in chapters 5 to 9 of the Book of I Kings. The work levy that Solomon raised was a 'tribute of bond-service' made up of 'all the people that were left of the Amorites, Hittites, Perizzites, Hivites and Jebusites which were not of the children of Israel'. Over these bondmen were 550 chief officers, the top administrators, and under these were 3,300 officers directing the work. The work force was in three divisions of which one was 30,000 men who were builders (they were building, not 'in Lebanon' as the translation has it). This building crew did not all work at once: 10,000 worked one month and had two months off so that at one out of every three months, any one man only worked four months out of the year. There was a second division of 70,000 men whose job was transport whether by hand or sledge or boat. The third division of 80,000 men was 'hewers in the mountains' supplying stone and logs. Herodotus is not far off with his 'a hundred thousand men labored constantly, and were relieved every three months by a fresh lot'.

I have already found the stepped pyramid appearing in translation in our Bibles as a stepped throne. So it would be reasonable to expect that the Great Pyramid appears also, disguised of course by errors of translation, and I do believe I have found the very thing in the first two sentences of Solomon's speech inaugurating the temple newly completed.

This speech dates from his eleventh year of sole rule, delivered after seven years of work, and so of course the pyramid was only well started. I would guess that the central core was built up far enough to support the lower chamber. Or perhaps he had gotten so far already as to have in place what is nowadays called the King's chamber. And so he explained to the assembled congregation just what he had in mind. He meant to build a place for God to 'abide in forever'. He well knew the temple would not abide forever. It lasted a little more than four hundred years. And so to find what he was talking about, all we have to do is look for something still there. And there it is, the Great Pyramid.

No one seems to know where the word 'pyramid' comes from. The same lack of derivation also applies to the Arabic word for pyramid which is haram. Haram, if you look it up in the Arabic dictionary, means feebleness, decrepitude and weakness and then, all of a sudden with no explanation, pyramid. But here at least I find the same associated meaning in what Solomon called the eternal abode of God at his inauguration of the temple. In chapter 8 of I Kings he says in the first sentence of his speech, 'The Lord said that he would dwell in the thick darkness'. In the next sentence Solomon says 'I have built a house zbl... '. This zbl in the Hebrew speech is the cognate Arabic dhbl which means feeble, decrepit and weak, the same as 'haram' means. So allow me to introduce, suddenly and with no explanation at all, the concept that zbl means also 'pyramid'. The English translation fudges this sentence so that it isn't clear the word is translated at all. In my Hebrew-English bilinear the translation is 'I have built a house of loftiness... '. But the Hebrew zbl is the Arabic dhbl which is the equivalent of 'haram' so that Solomon himself says 'I have built a house, a pyramid... '. Or, come to think of it, he was not referring to the Great Pyramid. When he made this speech he was called Sneferu and he had by this time finished the stepped pyramid. David, perhaps, indicated the site by saying that he would dwell in the house of the Lord forever and it was in the stepped pyramid that David, as Djoser, was laid to rest. This site may also be indicated by God's complaint to a prophet that His abode was defiled by the graves of the dead. Sometime after Hezekiah was interred there, the bodies were all moved to comply with God's complaint. This appears to have been done during the reign of the revivalist king Josiah who was shot down by Necho's archer. That's two hints that the eternal abode meant by Solomon in his speech is the stepped pyramid. There is a third hint.

There were three princesses of Misraim in Solomon's time. One married Solomon's enemy Hadad, another married Solomon and the third became the Queen of Misraim whom the Bible names Tahpenes. The Bible neglects to name this wife of Solomon's but it does name her daughter as Taphath. It says in II Chronicles chapter 8 that, after this wife died, Solomon 'brought up the daughter of pharaoh out of the city of David unto the house that he had built for her: for he said, My wife shall not dwell in the house of David King of Israel because the places are holy whereunto the ark of the Lord hath come'. So Solomon at first interred her in the precincts of the stepped pyramid but then later on changed his mind and moved her somewhere else. And right there in those precincts is her first grave – the courtyard and mausoleum of Hetepherabti. The Egyptologists seem to think that this was Djoser's daughter. I say this is his daughter-in-law, Solomon's wife. If the name does not simply mean 'the Abode of Hetepheres', then it means 'Hetepheres the Goddess' or some such honorific. The name Hetepheres is of a kind with Taphath her daughter and is very nearly the same name as Tahpenes, or Tahphenes, her sister. Hetepheres was the wife of Cheops and her grave has been found near the Great Pyramid. It is a shaft grave which the archaeologists judge to be a secondary burial. So now we know where Solomon moved her to. Even better, we know that the ark was lodged for a time within the compound of the stepped pyramid, the 'city of David'.

CHAPTER SIX

THE REAL RAMSES

IN THE FIRST CENTURY AD Josephus Flavius undertook to defend the Jews in his pamphlet *Contra Apion*. Apion was a rabble rouser who among other things charged the Jews with a Hyksos past. This did not get a rise out of Josephus. Of course the Hebrews were Hyksos, he said, since they invaded the country to rule and inhabit it. So there you are. Nobody bothered putting Hyksos in Palestine. The term applies only to Egypt and so both Apion and Josephus put the Kingdom of Israel solidly on the Nile. 'Hyksos' was a generic term that applied to any foreign people that conquered Egypt. Thus, strictly speaking, not only were the Hebrews and their time to time conquerors, Syrians and Assyrians, Hyksos, so were the Babylonians, and the Persians, and the Greeks, and the Romans and, most recently, the Arabs. It appears that the Syrians were the worst offenders, ripping up women with child as the Bible says. And in the ten years before Alexander came to the rescue, the vengeful Persians satisfied the worst definition of the term Hyksos with slaughters so gruesome that their own Jewish allies were embarrassed. And, according to Josephus, Ptolemy Soter, the Savior, who established the line of Ptolemies, might better be called Ptolemy the Destroyer for his slaughters of the people. And the invader Umar, the second caliph, ordered the Arabs to slay on sight every person who met a particular description. It was he, not Theodosius nor even Chosroes, who ended ancient Egypt forever.

The heart of Josephus' defense is a King List that he got from Manetho's history of Egypt, a surviving fragment which he introduces, says he, as though the Egyptian priest was raised from his grave to testify in the witness box. He quotes Manetho to say that in the days of the Egyptian King Timaeus the gods were so angry that they brought on a people coming from the east to invade and conquer the land. After some considerable time, this people made one of themselves a king whose name was Salitus.

Stop right there. Remember that Josephus was trying to defend the Jews in general and, in particular, he was trying to stop the Alexandrian lynch mobs from destroying the Jewish quarter. How could he have any hope of doing this unless he introduced evidence that wasn't just relevant to the quarrel but was obvious as well? The obvious thing is that Manetho refers to the invasion by Israel and then to the time of the judges that was ended with the coronation of Saul, the last ruler of the 2nd Dynasty. Manetho wrote in Greek so the names he gives are in Greek form. It appears to me that Salitus is a Greek form of Saul. I assume that Manetho's thirteen years for Salitus means that Judge Samuel died that long before Saul did. Only then was Saul free to rule alone. So, since David began to reign early in 1089 BC, Manetho starts his King List in the middle of 1102 BC. From there Manetho occupies the next 511 years with Hyksos rulers. The entire Old Kingdom in other words, Dynasties 3 through 6, is the Hyksos era according to Manetho! The last two of the six major Hyksos he names are Yunis and Isses. These same two appear in Grimal's 5th Dynasty as Wenis and Issesi just about where they should be on his inflated time scale.

This Hyksos era was ended by a 'long and terrible war'. We don't have to wonder who the protagonists of this war are; they are Nebuchadnezar and his armies and allies on the one side, and the King of Misraim and his armies and allies on the other. Babylonia and Misraim were neighbors, Misraim extending south and east of Babylonia. And as Babylonia's holdings were to the north in Assyria and west in Anatolia, Misraim's holdings were west in Syria and in Egypt. And so the contest was between the two great powers of the age. The last King of Israel, Zedekiah, threw in his lot with Psammetichus II, King of Misraim. They lost, and all their skilled and educated people in Egypt, in Israel, went into captivity. Only their poor and their farmers were left to till the fields. This captivity is what Manetho means by the eviction of the Hyksos. This time of revolution was bewailed by the Egyptian scribe who said that the maid who used to admire her face in a water puddle now admires herself in the mirror of her former mistress who now goes begging in the streets.

Manetho ends the 511 year Hyksos era with the Great War that broke out in the last quarter of 607 BC. He does not say how long the war lasted so let me guess at twenty years which would be about when Hophra, the last King of Misraim, was defeated. That brings Manetho's King List to a total of 531 years so far. Mind you, both Manetho and Josephus use the 354 day year, so here we are at circa 587 BC. With the final defeat of the Hyksos at about this time, Manetho introduces a dynasty lasting 327 years which lands us at circa 271 BC. And so this dynasty can only begin in the Babylonian era, continue through the Persian era and end during the reign of Ptolemy II Philadelphus, about the time that Manetho died. And so you'd expect that this King List of Manetho's should end here. But it doesn't! It carries on for more than a hundred years. How is that possible? Simple, Josephus updated it.

After Manetho's crisp reign lengths of so many years and so many months, Josephus suddenly goes obscure about the passage of time. And after Manetho's Greek style names, Josephus suddenly introduces two Egyptian style names, Sety and Ramses. The best I can tell, Josephus puts Sety 66 years after Manetho's last entry and then he ends Ramses 66 years after that. These are obviously not reign lengths. Josephus only means to place Sety and then Ramses accurately on the time scale. So let's play along with him and see what he is after. He places Sety late in 208 BC. Sety is Antiochus the Great! Josephus says that this Sety had a navy that threw his weight around the Mediterranean; that he campaigned east as far as India; and that he returned to throw out his 'brother' that had abused the Queen of Egypt. No Egyptologist has ever dared claim that their Sety, that's their Sety of the 19th Dynasty, ever went as far east as India. Or had a navy. Or returned from his campaigns to throw out an abusive caretaker brother and put Egypt under his protective custody. Only one man in all history ever did all that and that man is Antiochus III the Great. That brother of his, nicknamed Danaus by Josephus, appears to be Sosibius who didn't just abuse the queen of the playboy Ptolemy IV, he murdered her, and then he went into exile. Josephus then goes on to end Ramses 66 years later which would be in 144 BC. Guess what? That is about when Jonathan Maccabeus fought the battle of Qadesh unless it was a year earlier. This miraculous battle defines Ramses. Where that battle is, there will Ramses be. Josephus tells us all about it in chapter 5 of book 13 of his *Antiquities*.

In 145 BC there were two Seleucid claimants to the throne fighting each other not only for their domain of Mesopotamia and Syria but for control of Egypt as well. This control, or oversight at least, dated from the days of Antiochus the Great who had managed it in large part by his friendship and alliance with the Jews and so it was nothing out of the ordinary when these two claimants vied for Jonathan's support. Jonathan was at first allied with Demetrius who had promised in writing a tax exempt status for the Jews. But then, faced with the necessity of raising a large army to realize his ambitions, Demetrius reversed himself and demanded that the Jews pay not only current taxes but back taxes as well, and he added that if they did not pay up then it would be war. Faced with this treachery from the man that he had once saved from an Antioch lynch mob, Jonathan chose war. He switched his support to the son of the recently deceased Seleucid king, to the boy Antiochus, who turned over to him all the resources of Phoenicia and Palestine and Syria so long as he would fight for him. It was a deal. And so it happened that, no later than 144 BC, Jonathan set out on a recruitment and fund drive. Wars cost money.

Starting along the Mediterranean on the eastern border of Egypt, he and his private army went up the coast through Ashkelon recruiting allegiance and treasure. Everywhere, he was received in the cities 'splendidly indeed', says Josephus, except at Gaza which he had to siege before they changed their minds and agreed to a league of friendship. Everywhere he went through Phoenicia and

Palestine the roads were as safe and the people as welcoming as back home in his own bailiwick. Demetrius was not a popular man. When he reached Damascus though, he had to change his plans. Demetrius' generals, alarmed at Jonathan's progress, had raised a large army and driven south to the city of Qadesh where they were poised to invade Galilee. Their plan was that by threatening Galilee they would draw Jonathan out of Damascus and Syria into a trap. And it worked. Well, almost.

Fearing that Demetrius' army might already be ravaging Galilee, Jonathan left Damascus and marched west through the foothillsof Mt. Hermon. He camped in a square bivouac at 'the waters of Gennesar', the south edge of Lake Genneseret, the Sea of Galilee. Then, crossing the ford of the Jordan there and seeing the enemy was not that far south yet, he turned north searching all the way and crossed the north border of Galilee into the Plains of Hazor 'without knowing' that the enemy was there. This plain and Qadesh lay, says Josephus, in the borderland between Galilee and the hinterland of Tyre.

The ambush laid the day before was sprung. When Demetrius' army came charging from behind Qadesh, Jonathan's rearguard was already collapsing under surprise attack and he got ready 'as well as he was able' as Josephus says. As his lines were smashed behind him with the worst yet to come from in front, his whole army broke and ran except for two commanders, Mattathias and Judas, who stuck by him. Meanwhile, an elite corps sent from Tyre arrived on the scene but before they could do anything Jonathan and his two friends did something unheard of in the history of warfare. They, three men alone, attacked a whole army. Such was their reckless fury and deadly affect that Demetrius' army, in their thousands, began to retreat back to the safety of the walls of Qadesh. The corps from Tyre joined the fray and those that had run away now came running back and Demetrius' generals lost two thousand dead on their way to slam the gates of the fortress and peer in safety through the battlements at a man who appeared to be possessed by the God of Battle. That man, Jonathan, broke off and returned without trying to take the city. Why should he bother? He had upstaged all the heroes of old. All he had to do now was sit still and wait for men and treasure to come to him.

Here without mistake are all the defining elements of the battle of Qadesh as the Egyptologists tell it, speaking of Ramses II of the 19th Dynasty and that supposed battle of his: the applauded tour from the coast to Damascus involving a siege along the way; the sudden change from the tour to hunting the enemy fox in the region of Lebanon; the trap sprung by that enemy in front and behind; the runaway army; the elite corps from the coast; and one man putting the run on a whole army that ran for safety back to the fortress of Qadesh. This story is engraved in stone in the hieroglyphics on the walls of Karnak. Aside from the embroidery of court poets, death rays shooting from the helmet of the hero for instance, the Egyptologists only get one thing wrong: it wasn't his two horses that Ramses rewarded with a perpetual invite to his table; it was his two army chiefs. In the old language, the word for warhorse and for chief was almost the same. Either the Egyptologists make a mistake in translation, or Ramses II, who is Constantine the Great who stole the story, altered the tale because he loved his horses more than his fellowman.

Hazor is also called Tell el Qadeh and this Qadeh as Qada' means to be elapsed or expired or old. Since I have never seen anything of archaeological significance from the place called Qadesh nearby to the north, the conventional site of Jonathan's battle, I believe Hazor is the authentic site of Qadesh the Old of the monuments describing the battle. Tell el Qadeh has been excavated and with the rock eminence at the south edge with the fortress perched on top and the horseshoe wall and moat round the city with its heels resting on the fortress, and the stream that used to wrap round the fortress on three sides, and the reservoir pond within the walls at the foot of the fortress, and the little lake Hul nearby to the east, it all fits well enough the picture of the battle scene carved in stone at Karnak. It is striking how well that picture matches the aerial photo of the excavated remains of Hazor.

Only before this battle, when Josephus mentions the Roman army style square formation used by Jonathan, the same formation pictured at Karnak, and after it, when Demetrius' generals tried again and again failed after Jonathan's scouts captured the spies, the same spies of the Karnak story, did Jonathan campaign north of Lebanon in the region of Homs where the historians suppose the battle was. And so three different rivers would feature in Jonathan's campaigns: the Litani and the Jordan that drained south Lebanon, one west and one east of Hazor; and the Orontes that drained north Lebanon to run by Homs. Meanwhile, Egyptian texts telling the story of Ramses show three different names for three different rivers. One of these is read by the Egyptologists as the Orontes. The only trouble with that is that the river was never called that until the Persian era of the 6th century BC when a Persian named Orontes arranged an ingenious crossing for the Persian army.

And so it is that Antiochus the Great and Jonathan Maccabeus are the original Sety and Ramses. Their reputations were usurped almost 500 years later by Diocletian and Constantine, the Egyptologists' Sety and Ramses II of the 19th Dynasty. And indeed the Egyptologists report that the star chart in the tomb of Ramses II gives a date 500 years older than it should be. That's because either Constantine usurped Jonathan's tomb or he found that tomb and copied all its texts.

It would be tedious and something interesting only to scholars to show that Jonathan died in 140 BC and that Manetho's Orus, of that dynasty that Egyptologists take to be the 18th, is none other than the great Persian satrap Arsames who began to reign over Egypt in 430 BC or a year later, and that Manetho's Armies Miamun towards the end of that same dynasty is none other than Seleucus dead circa 281 BC. Suffice it to say that now we can understand just what Josephus had in mind when he defended the Jews in *Contra Apion*. It might not be enough to stop an Alexandrian mob in its tracks but it was enough to make a fair minded person think twice. He couldn't very well say what he knew since the hostile audience would not have accepted that. And so he offered what that audience could accept, Manetho's own testimony that invaded the Nile Valley with Israel and started the greater Hyksos with King Saul. These greater Hyksos occupied almost half of the 511 year Hyksos era of the Old Kingdom. Manetho names these greater Hyksos, giving their reigns precisely, so many years, so many months. There are six of them, and those reign lengths are enough to reveal their identity. They are Saul, David, Solomon, and Shishak from Misraim in Mesopotamia, and then the two Syrians Hadad and Hazael. Manetho does not bother to name the lesser Hyksos but they are obviously Assyrians and Psammetichides. The most obvious of the Assyrians is Pepy II of the

6th Dynasty who is none other than Ashurbanipal. There is a reason for 6th Dynasty statuary looking Assyrian – it is Assyrian. I have already shown that Nitocris ending that dynasty is the Psammetichide Nitocris dead circa 589 BC. She ends Manetho's Hyksos era well into his 'long and terrible war'. Remember, I only guessed this might have been a twenty year war. That's a little short. Make it twenty-four years and some months to extend Manetho's sequence just enough so that the 66 years that Josephus gives Ramses ends in 140 BC when Jonathan died. If you follow back Josephus' King List of the Maccabees, he ends him in 140 BC not in the conventional 142 BC.

Since the Manetho-Josephus King List bridges all the time from the end of the 6th Dynasty to sometime within the 13th and 14th Dynasties, I am going to leave it at that just to keep things simple and jump, in the following chapter, to the 18th Dynasty. In the Introduction I have already shown that the 15th and 16th Dynasties, the Egyptologist's Hyksos, are Greco Romans and Romans starting about the time that the Roman general drew the line in the sand and that the 17th Dynasty is that of Herod.

One last thing before I leave this List. The Egyptologists quote old Greek and Latin authors as though they mention Ramses. Of course if they did then I would be wrong to say Jonathan is the original. But I am not wrong because those authors invariably name Armies, or Armeeses, Miamun who is either Seleucus I or Ptolemy I Soter. The Egyptologists make the mistake of assuming that Manetho's Armies or Armeeses is a form of the name Ramses. Of course it's not. Ramses is Jonathan Maccabeus and Armies is one of the two greatest companions of Alexander the Great.

CHAPTER SEVEN

THE ANTONINES OF THE 18TH DYNASTY

AN EGYPTIAN SCRIBE TRACED THE CIVIL WAR leading up to the 18th Dynasty back to the tyrant Apophis in northern Egypt who sent a message to Seqenenre, a southern governor, saying that he couldn't sleep for the noise of the people and demanding that everyone stay away from the pool of the hippopotamus. That, anyway, is how the Egyptologists translate it. Since the governor's response was grief and a stunned silence, it appears the message was somehow an affront but I don't know how the Egyptologists arrive at the conclusion that it was the product of an unbalanced mind. After all, why shouldn't a perfectly sane man complain that unruly crowds were keeping him awake? What's wrong with that? And why shouldn't he order people to leave the hippopotamuses alone? Maybe they were an endangered species. Maybe this Apophis was the world's first ecologically conscious ruler. Nonetheless, I agree with the Egyptologists. The man was insane. He was Caligula.

Only here, nowhere else, the Egyptologists introduce a

demented insomniac. And I expected they would do this because this is that time in Roman history when a demented insomniac occurs for the first and only time. This Apophis that the Egyptologists take to be a Hyksos of the 15th or 16th Dynasty is none other than Caligula.

And then there's this hippo business. The hippopotamus is the river horse and in the old language the word for river horse and for a smooth running race horse is about the same word. And the word for pool and for an enclosure, or stable, is about the same word. And so the Egyptologists' 'pool of the hippopotamus' should probably be 'stable of my racehorse'. Stay away from the stable of my racehorse, Caligula said. He didn't want people bothering his favorite candidate for senator.

Caligula was assassinated under a rain of blows that started when he was standing and ended as he lay prostrate. The Latin author Suetonius mentions two of the wounds delivered while he was standing. One of these was a stab in the back of the neck and the other was a smash in the face. We have what is said to be the mummy of Seqenenre who died under a rain of blows, two of which match the ones mentioned by Suetonius. Since mummies were sometimes misidentified by the old Egyptian priests in the course of moving them around, there is the possibility that this is the body of Apophis, Caligula, rather than Seqenenre whoever that was. The age is right, it is the body of a young man, and the lineage is right, it is that of an old family type. Harris and Weeks, in their *X-Raying the Pharaohs*, say that the facial complex resembles more the Old Kingdom Giza skull type than it does that of later Egyptian kings. Caligula was a Claudian, a very old lineage, and the Julio Claudians ceased in 68 AD with Nero. Nor is there any reason that the body of a supposed Hyksos might not have been preserved. The Egyptologists are perplexed that these 'Hyksos' appear to have enjoyed amicable relations with everybody contrary to what Manetho said of his Hyksos. What we need is a more complete list of Caligula's wounds and a match-up of those with those of the mummy.

Following Seqenenre, Grimal jumps immediately to the two brothers Kamose and Ahmose. This is not quite right. Budge, in his Hieroglyphic Dictionary, lists several rulers that can only be Claudius, Nero, Galba, Otho, Vitellius and Vespasian, before he gets to the two brothers, the sons of Vespasian who died in 79 AD. His son Titus died two years later and Domitian in 96 AD. But this doesn't matter. What matters is that after Apophis and Seqenenre, Caligula and whoever, the Egyptologists start the 18th Dynasty with two brothers, Kamose and Ahmose, just when Roman history puts the two brothers Titus and Domitian before the Antonines. Kamose can only be Titus and Ahmose can only be Domitian. The Egyptologists say these two brothers evicted the 'Hyksos' and so they did. Titus and Domitian evicted the Jews and destroyed the Roman aristocracy as well as the remnants of the Julio Claudians. Grimal says that Ahmose reigned 26 years. That's not bad. That would be Domitian for 26 years from 70 AD to his death in 96 AD. It was his father who began to reign in 70 AD but Domitian claimed that he was the rightful ruler and that his father and brother were his regents standing in for him because of his youth and so he himself claimed he reigned 26 years.

The rumor was that Domitian poisoned his elder brother such was his envy and hatred. And sure enough, the body of Kamose collapsed into a pile of scrap and dust when it was examined some years ago. Obviously, his brother Ahmose disposed of the body quickly without proper mummification. He did this to hide the fact that Titus was poisoned. The embalmers knew all about the symptoms of poisoning. They were the coroners of the day. We don't have to wonder about this. Test that pile of bones and dust and see if it doesn't show traces of some poison or other. The poison is probably of a sort that would leave obvious symptoms. Otherwise Domitian would not have buried the body so fast.

Ahmose was the second of two brothers; he buried his brother too fast to be honest; he laid the foundations of the 18th Dynasty. And he occurs in Egyptology exactly where I expect him to occur. It was Domitian who was those things and did those things and we don't have to argue about this. It can be proved. There is his mummy right there in Cairo beautifully preserved while his brother's body is a pile of garbage. Domitian was assassinated and Suetonius, in his *The Twelve Caesars*, describes the body in a clinical manner. The body is that of a man 45 years of age. He was tall, bald and well formed except for his feet which had hammer toes. He had a festering wart on his forehead and his legs were spindly from a long illness. He was slain by five attackers, with eight stab wounds, the first in the groin, and his fingers were slashed from grabbing a dagger blade. If I'm right and Suetonius is accurate and if the mummy is that of Ahmose, these marks of assassination underneath the thick layer of resin that Harris and Weeks say covers the body will prove that this Ahmose is Domitian. Suetonius says that long illness weakened Domitian. Harris and Weeks say the last years of Ahmose's life must have been very painful with arthritis so much in his knees and back that movement must have been difficult. He had by omen the day and hour of the attempt on his life. It was to be the fifth hour of the night but when he asked the time he was

THE ANTONINES OF THE 18TH DYNASTY

told it was the sixth hour and so, thinking the danger was past, he was off guard.

Ahmose finished what his brother Kamose had started against the 'Hyksos' and laid the foundations of the 18th-Dynasty, organizing its machinery of state. That's what Domitian did. He drove the old Roman aristocratic families to the point of extinction and to escape his persecutions the Jews fled the country. Then he laid the legal foundations of the autocratic regime of the Antonines, a regime in which the Senate was tolerated only to maintain the fiction of a republic.

After Ahmose, Grimal introduces Amenhotep I who was guided in the first part of his career by his mother in a sort of regency. In the Roman List, Domitian was followed by Nerva, an old man dead two years later, and then by Trajan, dead in 117 AD, who promoted his nephew Hadrian who had been guided in the first part of his career, during the reign of Domitian, by his mother. And the Egyptologists give Amenhotep I a reign of 21 years. It was Hadrian who reigned 21 years from 117 to 138 AD. And so it follows that Egyptology's Amenhotep I is Hadrian. He died of natural causes. His mummy is there in Cairo. Take a look at it. It shows no wounds of assassination. Furthermore, Harris and Weeks say that his mummy yielded on examination the smell of a certain flower. Now we know why. Hadrian died among friends and was succeeded by a friend. Had he been assassinated, he would have been followed by an enemy and nobody would have dared leave flowers in his grave. Incidentally, the Egyptological date for his death is circa 1500 BC. I'd like to see a scientist prove that a floral aroma could survive thirty-five hundred years in the enclosed atmosphere of a decaying mummy. I doubt any such smell could survive since 138 AD. Somebody probably put those flowers there long after he died. He was the beneficiary of a cult following and some of his poetry was passable.

After Amenhotep I, the Egyptologists come to what they call the difficulties of the Thutmoside succession. They are pretty sure but not certain of who belongs on the list and of who follows who. And sure enough it is just here that we come to the complex arrangements that Hadrian made for his succession. I find that the Egyptologists have done a good job since all the people they mention are recognizable but they do make two mistakes: Thutmose IV belongs after, not before, Amenhotep III as we shall see, and Thutmose I that they put after Amenhotep I does not belong on the list since he died before Amenhotep I did.

Just when the Egyptologists expect the body of Thutmose I, Amenhotep's successor, to be that of a man at least in his fifties, they find instead the body of what appears to be an eighteen year old. If that age estimate is correct then what we have here is Pedanius Fuscas who was the only one to die young that had anything to do with succeeding Hadrian. A faction advanced him as Hadrian's successor around 134 AD but he was executed two years later.

The estimate of eighteen years is on the grounds that Thutmose I's bones do not have the closure of maturity. But Harris and Weeks say that he had rheumatoid arthritis which prevents bone closure. So there is no reason why this Thutmose I cannot be the thirty-eight year old Verus I who was adopted by Hadrian as successor in 136 AD but then died of natural causes in 138 AD, a few months before Hadrian did. This identification is that much the more likely since the body is completely bald, a condition that might be expected in a thirty-eight year old playboy who had drunk more than his share of leaded wine, and since there is a family resemblance between Thutmose I and Thutmose II. The Egyptologists assume they are father and son and I think they are right since Verus I was Verus II's father. So, since the Verus succession after Hadrian matches the Thutmoside succession after Amenhotep I, it follows that Thutmose I is Verus I.

This adoption business was started by Nerva, an old man already in 96 AD when he succeeded Domitian. Nerva, seeing he had not long to live, immediately adopted Trajan, and Trajan, on his deathbed so the story goes, adopted Hadrian. Seen in its best light, the idea of adoption was that the successor be chosen on grounds of competence rather than merely because of a family connection. Rome now meant to avoid dynastic wildcards of the likes of Caligula and Nero, and of Domitian for that matter. With this precedent to go on, Hadrian adopted Verus I, a shaky choice in itself but a choice justified by the idea that two very likely boys would be his true successors. These boys were Verus II, eight years old at the time and the natural son of Verus I, andVerus III, Annius Verus, who came to be known as Marcus Aurelius who was eighteen years old at the time. Whatever Hadrian's failings might be, and he certainly had them, he overcame them in the choice of his eventual successor, Verus III, Marcus Aurelius, the Philosopher King who was almost perfect in all his ways. But at the moment, Hadrian was stymied. Verus I died before his time and so Hadrian was stuck with two boys too young to conduct the affairs of state. And so he adopted a caretaker, Antoninus Pius, a man in his forties, who should reign until the two boys were old enough. And so, on adopting Antoninus as his successor, he required that Antoninus immediately adopt as his successors Verus II and Verus III. What he did not foresee was that Faustina

Younger, the natural daughter of Antoninus and Faustina Elder, Marcus Aurelius' aunt, would claim the throne in her own right, which she did. And so we have all the makings, in the history of Rome, of the complications of the Thutmoside succession. The man that the Egyptologists expected to find in Thutmose I, a man in his fifties, is Antoninus Pius. He does not appear in the King List because he was a caretaker. Instead, Thutmose I, II and III are Verus I, II and III. And Hatshepsut Elder and Younger are Faustina Elder and Younger. Faustina Elder was the wife of Antoninus and her daughter Faustina Younger was the stepsister and wife of Marcus Aurelius, Thutmose III.

The Egyptologist Brugsch-Bey says that Thutmose III cut in stone at Syene the words speaking of his wife Hatshepsut Younger: 'What I relate is no invention. She was astonishing in the sight of men and a secret for the hearts of the gods who knew all. But she was unaware of all this because she was not conscious of herself'. Spoken like a philosopher. That is Marcus Aurelius talking, a copy of his speech to the Senate proposing the deification of his wife Faustina Younger. The Senate approved his proposal which is why his words are cut in stone at the temple built in her honor at Syene.

The Egyptologists say that Thutmose III died on the 17th of March in 1425 BC. That's all we need to know to identify him. That date is the 1605th anniversary, backwards, of Marcus Aurelius' death. Marcus Aurelius is the one who died on the 17th of March. Only it was in 180 AD. That's exactly 1605 years later. The Egyptologists for once have gotten their seasonally adjusted dates exactly right. I have already shown that those dates of theirs play out in real time on a 1605 year cycle, and that their only serious error is stopping a cycle high.

The Egyptologists put Amenhotep II after Thutmose III and here, not before and not after, the King of Egypt goes on record as the peerless archer. That is enough to prove his identity because only here, not before or after in Roman history, does a Roman emperor go on record as the peerless archer. The man is Commodus, the son of Marcus Aurelius. Gibbon describes his feats. He strikes a panther in mid-leap. He decapitates an ostrich in full stride with a crescent shaped arrow head. He looses one arrow after another so fast he could easily star in Buffalo Bill's Wild West Show. Commodus learned this extraordinary skill from Moors and Parthians who taught him to 'dart the javelin and to shoot with the bow' and he soon equaled the most skillful of his teachers. Had he kept this skill to the battlefield and the hunt he might have escaped the wrath of Gibbon who, following the Latin authors, condemns him for entertaining the circus crowd at the expense of imperial dignity. But sure enough, the Latin authors were right. Commodus was soon guilty of conduct unbecoming an officer and a gentleman: he fought as a swordsman against net and trident men hundreds of times and his circus achievements were ordered to be recorded in the public acts of the empire which is why, in the case of Amenhotep II, such feats appear in hieroglyphics on the Nile that used to only record the deeds of battle. It was Amenhotep's boast that no man could pull his bow and nobody could hit his targets. That's what Commodus said.

Commodus was compared to Hercules and there is in the Capitolina Museum at Rome a marble bust showing him as Hercules peering out from a lion's head, his visage framed in its jaws. This sculpture is much too bland to do him justice. He looks like a playboy going to a masked ball. A much better likeness is the untitled sphinx dug up somewhere in Egypt that showsa man's face as true to life as the Greek sculptor could make it but instead of the striped headdress of the King there is the great bushy mane of the lion that appears to actually grow from the man's head and neck. The face is grim, the gaze bleak, as though looking out on the field of the slain. I read somewhere that he found this representation embarrassing, perhaps because some Latin authors mocked him for looking out on a field of slain bottles and wine jugs. But there it is. This sphinx is Commodus Amenhotep II wearing the lion's mane and whoever carved it must have witnessed his combats and seen him close up many times.

Not since Domitian does the work of the assassin again provide a means of identification. No stab wounds here. Commodus was strangled says Lampridius in *Lives of the Later Caesars*. His wine was spiked and as he lay in a stupor, a wrestler, a sparring partner of his, came in and throttled him. Harris and Weeks show a side-view X-ray photo of the head and neck of Amenhotep II. It appears that his larynx has been crushed and pushed up under his jaw. His sparring partner did that in 192 AD.

CHAPTER EIGHT

THE PSEUDO ANTONINES OF THE 18TH DYNASTY

COMMODUS WAS THE LAST OF THE ANTONINES. Well, sort of. Caracalla claimed that Commodus was his father not Septimius Severus his supposed father who succeeded Commodus and reigned from 192 to 211 AD. The Antonines were held in such high esteem, because of 'the five good emperors' Nerva, Trajan, Hadrian, Antoninus Pius and Marcus Aurelius, that anyone claiming to be one of them could count on popular support. And so Caracalla gained a popularity that he would not have otherwise enjoyed. People accepted his claim that he was an Antonine because it was a fact that he much resembled Commodus. The only difference was in their size. Commodus was powerfully built while Caracalla was small and weak. And there he is, Thutmose IV the son of Amenhotep II. Harris and Weeks, examining their mummies, noted the resemblance of their faces. Their physiques though differed. The son must have been small and weak compared to his father.

Nor can there be any doubt about who Amenhotep III

is. He was crippled toward the last of his reign by being, as the historians say, diseased in his feet. All the kings had their aches and pains but only here, in all Egyptology, and just where I expect it does one have trouble with his feet. Septimius Severus was crippled toward the last of his reign by being, as the historians say, diseased in his feet. In all Roman history, only here does an emperor's feet get into the public record. So crippled was he at last that the army, on his postponing a campaign, wanted to make Caracalla co-ruler.

The Egyptologists list Amenhotep II and then Thutmose IV and then Amenhotep III. That is, they list Commodus, then Caracalla and then Septimius as though Caracalla was Septimius' father and predecessor. How could they make a mistake like that? I think it comes from what historians recognize as the post mortem adoption of Septimius Severus by Marcus Aurelius. Since Marcus was dead, the rite of adoption could only have been carried out by an Antonine other than Marcus and the only one living at the time was Caracalla. I find the record of this adoption carved on the wall of Amenhotep's court at Luxor where the gist of the text reads that the god Thutmose III appeared in the guise of Thutmose IV who approached the Queen lying on her couch. The result was that an already grown Amenhotep III was 'born' of the 'union'. In other words, Marcus Aurelius appeared in the guise of Caracalla who approached the Queen Julia Domne who was Septimius Severus' wife. And then Septimius probably passed between her legs in the manner of the ancient rite and so was 'born' an Antonine the 'son' of Marcus Aurelius. Certainly not the 'son' of Caracalla. The Egyptologists read the text as a seduction scene recording the moment of the conception of Amenhotep III. The Latin authors seemed to prefer the tale of incest between Caracalla and his stepmother. Spartianus says in *Lives of the Later Caesars* that it is of interest to know how Caracalla seduced his stepmother, or she him. At his advance, she says 'If you wish it, it is permitted'. Carved in stone on the wall at Luxor she says 'What is thy will?' which amounts to the same thing. It is as though Spartianus, touring Egypt, read the same hieroglyphics as have the Egyptologists.

The Egyptologists say that Amenhotep III accounts for more buildings and monuments than any other ruler of ancient times and his reign, benefitting from the wars of Thutmose III and Amenhotep II, marks the peak of wealth, peace and prosperity in Egypt. At the same time, the historians of Rome say that Septimius Severus accounts for more buildings and monuments than any other emperor and his peace, bought with the wars of Marcus Aurelius and the arbitrary justice of Commodus, ushered the empire to a peak of wealth and prosperity. But not only do his feet and peaceful wealth single out Amenhotep III to be Severus, just as unique is his unprecedented connections with Syria. The Egyptologists trace his in-laws as well as his solar rites of the Aten to Syria. Here again, it was Septimius Severus who found his wife, Julia Domne, in Syria and she brought her relatives along and seduced the Roman Caesar, as Gibbon says, to the effeminate practices of the east.

After Septimius Severus died, the empire was divided with Egypt going to Geta, Caracalla's brother. Caracalla wanted Egypt too, but his brother stood in the way. The Egyptological tale goes that Thutmose IV was ahunting when he rested by the Sphinx and dreamed that the god told him that if he cleared away the heap (of sand), then he would reign over Egypt. However, I find in Budge's *Hiero-*

glyphic Dictionary that 'geta', among other things, means a 'heap' or 'pile'. So now we know how to read that stele of Thutmose IV there at the Sphinx. It means that Caracalla dreamed that his ambition was confirmed when the shade of Marcus Aurelius appeared to tell him that if he cleared away Geta (his brother, not sand), then he would reign over Egypt. And that is what Caracalla did. A year after Septimius Severus died, Caracalla slew his brother and reigned five years 'til 217 AD.

Harris and Weeks X-ray photo of Thutmose IV's head and neck shows a bone structure almost girlish compared to that of Amenhotep II to which it is compared. Harris and Weeks say the body of Thutmose IV is that of a thin weak fellow who died at about thirty years of age. That is true since Caracalla died at the age of twenty-nine and was said to have been of small size and so weak from his dissolute life that he could not bear the weight of the cuirass on a march of any length. So accurate so far, Harris and Weeks go wandering off the track. They say '...the large and rather crude incision made in the abdomen by the embalmers suggests a hasty and even rather unprofessional job of mummification...' and they show a picture of this. It is a jagged-edged opening about six inches long from his left side to the middle of his stomach and about four inches wide. This is no embalmer's incision which was always sewn closed. It is a gaping wound. It is a disemboweling cut delivered from the left. For the third time in this line of emperors, the assassin has left a mark for purposes of identification.

As Caracalla rode east of Antioch towards Carrhea and the Temple of the Moon, he stopped to relieve himself and as he went to mount up, his equerry, say the Latin authors, stabbed him in the side killing him. As Caracalla lifted his hands to the horse's saddle, the equerry stepped in under his left arm and thrust him through the belly and ripped him up, disemboweling him. The embalmers discarded the hanging flap and could not sew the wound closed. Just before he was slain, he was likely humming to himself the latest ditty, the song to the Moon goddess in the do-re-mi scale on a clay tablet that the archaeologists dug up near Antioch a few years ago.

In the sculptor's workshop at Akhetaten the archaeologists dug up the bust of a man in the same strata as that of the bust of Nefertiti. At least one Egyptologist has commented that this man looks just like Caracalla. That's because it is Caracalla. There are extant sculptures of him and this one belongs in that collection. There is a reason that this bust was found there in the city that Akhenaten built. Akhenaten is none other than Heliogabalus who claimed that Caracalla was his father, so naturally the bust would have been commissioned.

Akhenaten and his reign was signed by a trademark ideogram – the sun with its rays and at the end of each ray a hand offering a loaf of bread, the staff of life. This ideogram translates as Heliogabalus. 'Helio' means the sun and 'gabalus' is from the trilateral root jbl meaning, besides a mountain, to create, make or offer something. Akhenaten's ideogram reads as the life offering sun and so he signs his name as Heliogabalus, the rayed sun offering life to the multitudes. But his contemporaries had another name for him. They called him a wretch and a criminal. And the Egyptologists record those same terms of opprobrium just here where I expect them to because it is just here that the Latin authors call Heliogabalus the same thing.

Only once in ancient Egypt did an emperor push the boundaries of depravity and at the same time attempt to impose the Sun God of Syria, of Homs, on everybody. All you have to do to know Akhenaten was depraved is look at his statues, pictures of them. They feature a vacant crotch. No sign of male genitalia there. Now we know why. Lampridius, in *Lives of the Later Caesars*, tells us that Heliogabalus 'tied up his genitals' in the manner of devotees of the cult of Salambo that required either that or castration and practiced child sacrifice as a means of divination. '... he celebrated the rite of Salambo with all the wailing and frenzy of the Syrian cult (and) sacrificed human victims having chosen for this boys that were noble, their parents living... he inspected (for the oracle) the children's innards (after the manner of) his own native ritual'. He also sent agents to prowl the bathhouses to recruit his paramours, men of a particular description. So those Egyptologists are right who suspect that Akhenaten indulged in that sort of thing.

The Egyptologists say that Akhenaten's agenda was to make the Syrian Sun God and its priesthood paramount in Egypt. That's what they mean by his monotheism and they are right because that was Heliogabalus' agenda. He violated the sanctity of the Roman temples to carry away their most sacred symbols in order to put them under the control of his priesthood. According to Lampridius, he also proposed that the religion of the Jews and Samaritans and the rites of the Christians ought to be transferred 'so that the priesthood of Heliogabalus might include the mysteries of every cult'. So now we know where that so called poem of Akhenaten comes from that so much resembles a certain Psalm. It does not anticipate the Psalms as the Egyptologists claim; it plagiarizes the Psalm. His idea was to demonstrate that the Psalm works as a poem in praise of the Syrian Sun God rather than the God of the Bible. I

THE PSEUDO ANTONINES OF THE 18TH DYNASTY

doubt he ever wrote those words. It was most likely done by some drudge in his employ. I don't doubt that he said the words, passed on by the Egyptologists, that he was accused of things worse than anything in his father's time, things worse than anything in his grandfather's time. Of course. He, Heliogabalus, was the worst thing to happen to Egypt up to then.

The Egyptologists take note of Akhenaten's leveling practices. This too is right. Rome's tyrants always bypassed the upper and middle classes to find their support in the mobs. As Lampridius says of Heliogabalus, 'He appointed freedmen as governors, legates, consuls and generals, and defiled every office with low born profligates'.

And there is the art of the Amarna era, the time around Akhenaten's reign. All of a sudden, things are drawn true to life. Wild fowl suddenly look like wild fowl. And the King's statue leaves the old formal style and suddenly looks just like the King, Akhenaten, in all his ugliness. Why this change just now? That's because, as Lampridius says, Heliogabalus ordered that what was before simulated in art, should now actually be done. Lampridius implies that this order meant that plays that involved rape and murder must actually do those things. However that may be, at least painting and sculpture display a modern sort of realism. (This was nothing new. Some sculptures from the Assyrian era of the 6th Dynasty may as well live and breathe.)

And there is that group of five women that start to show up, in Amenhotep III's reign, with Yuya and his wife Thuya. This Yuya was called the Divine Father and the Master of Horse. They had two daughters Tiy I and Tiy II. Tiy I was the wife of Amenhotep III. Tiy II, married to Ay I, had two daughters, Nefertiti and Mutnodjmet. Nefertiti's son was Tutankhamen and Mutnodjmet's was Akhenaten.

The Egyptologists make a hash of all this but I've got it right. We have a one to one correspondence here.

Yuya, perhaps Yahya or John or Johannes, is Bassianus Sun Priest of Homs which is Emesa just north of the Lebanese mountains on the Orontes River. His mummy is one of the best preserved ever, complete with a golden seal over the abdominal incision. Harris and Weeks describe his hair as red-gold, but in their color photo his hair looks like spun gold, and likewise his wife Thuya's mummy and her hair. They are, both of them, a veritable Goldilocks. Yuya also exhibits a large hawk nose and a most complacent expression, the look of one who died a satisfied man. These are not Syrians. What we have here are exhibits A and B, Yuya and Thuya, of what ancient Macedonians actually looked like. His priestly line was descended unwatered from the time of Alexander the Great if not earlier. These are 'children of the Sun', named for their golden hair as well as for their priesthood in the rites of the Sun.

Bassianus and his wife, whose name might have been Theodora, had two daughters, Julia Domne the wife of Septimius Severus, and Julia Maesa the wife of Avitus I. Julia Domne is Tiy I and Julia Maesa is Tiy II, while Avitus I is Ay I. Julia Maesa in turn had two daughters, Julia Mammea and Julia Soaemias, and one son Avitus II. Julia Mammea is Nefertiti, Julia Soaemias is Mutnodjmet and Avitus II is Ay II. Julia Mammea had a son, Alexander Severus, who is Tutankhamen and Julia Soaemias had a son, Heliogabalus, who is Akhenaten. Meanwhile, the Egyptologists' Smenkare must be Macrinus the pretender to the throne whose hopes were dashed in 218 AD by the army of Bassianus who ensured the reign of his grandson Heliogabalus. Leave it to the Egyptologists to turn 'Macrinus' into Smenkare' practically the same name. This victory of Bassianus is reported by the Egyptologists as a victory won by Akhenaten, his only claim to martial fame.

Avitus II is the Ay that the Egyptologists put as successor to Tutankhamen for four years. Actually, he was caretaker while Tutankhamen was away on campaign. That is to say, Avitus II took care of things while his nephew, Alexander Severus, campaigned against the up and coming Sassanids. The Egyptologists suspect that Tutankhamen was assassinated. They are right. The Latin authors say that Alexander Severus was murdered in his tent in the midst of his war but they don't seem to know exactly how it was done. Now we do. One examination of Tutankhamen's mummy mentions damage to the skull at the ear and that he must have died of cerebral bleeding. Another mentions an ice pick sized hole at the ear. So that is how Alexander Severus died before his time in 236 AD. There is an image of Tutankhamen leaning on his staff. This is an Egyptian version of the scene so often pictured on Greek pottery of the Homeric hero at ease leaning on his staff. This heroic ideal was very popular in the time of Alexander Severus.

And then there is Akhenaten's foreign policy which was to do nothing while the empire era Hittites, under a sly fellow the Egyptologists call Abdi Ashirta, invaded the Levant and Syria and Anatolia. That's what Heliogabalus did. He did nothing while the Sassanids overthrew the Arsacides and, under Ardishir, invaded the Levant and Syria and Anatolia to contest Roman control. Abdi Ashirta is Ardishir, the one who founded, by 230 AD, the Sassanide Empire of the Parthians.

And finally there is the fact that the Egyptologists have not found Akhenaten's body. Lampridius explains why. The fish in the River Tiber ate it. The soldiers, infuriated at last by his order that his young cousin Alexander be executed, slew Heliogabalus instead in the latrines where he was hiding. At first they tried flushing his body down the latrine sewer but it wouldn't go. So they dragged it round the circus to the delight of the crowds and then through the streets to the river where they pitched it in.

The Egyptologists end the 18th Dynasty with Horemhab reigning about thirty years after the end of Tutankhamen and Ay. Since Alexander Severus died around 236 AD, that means that Horemhab died circa 266 AD. Make that 268 AD, the year that Odenathus, governor of all the east and Egypt, died. In Egyptology, Horemhab is an obscure figure whose obscure thirty years also appears in Lampridius' account. Lampridius does not bother to name anyone between the death of Alexander Severus and the accession in 268 AD of Claudius Gothicus, Constantine's uncle. I can only guess that Horemhab is Odenathus whose defeat of the Sassanides saved Egypt. It is said that Horemhab served in the armies of Akhenaten and Tutankhamen. The reigning Caesar, Gallienus also dead in 268 AD, was too young to have been in the armies of Heliogabalus and Alexander. Only Odenathus could have done that.

CHAPTER NINE

RAMSES II IS CONSTANTINE

JUST ABOUT THE ONLY REASON to identify Ramses I beginning the 19th Dynasty as Claudius Gothicus, 268 to 270 AD, is because he was the one who was credited with starting the dynasty of Constantine. He was his uncle. And just about the only reason to say the next ruler Sety must be Diocletian is because Sety started an era, a 'repetition of births', which is what Diocletian did. As Lampridius says, Diocletian was the father of a golden age which refers to a Sothic cycle of 1605 years.

The Egyptologists do include some events in Sety's reign that are familiar, some of which actually occurred before he wielded sole power. For instance, the great triumph supposedly celebrated in his reign is the great triumph celebrated by Aurelian, 270 to 275 AD, not by Diocletian who began to reign nine years later. This was around 274 AD in memorial of Aurelian's conquest of Palmyra in Syria. It appears that Diocletian, Sety, co-opted the achievements of his predecessors the way that Constantine, Ramses II, did later on. The Egyptologists say this was the greatest triumph ever in ancient Egypt and that is what the Latin authors say about the triumph of Aurelian. Included in the parade was the prisoner of honor Zenobia Queen of Palmyra and widow of Odenathus. Incidentally, this title of hers doesn't necessarily mean she lived in Palmyra any more than Victoria's title Empress of India means she lived there. Zenobia had caused the war and her own downfall by her betrayal of Rome when she wrote to the Sassanide King that he send her a prince to marry which amounted to a proposal of alliance. That King did send a prince but he never got there. Aurelian showed up instead to pull down her walls and take her captive, which he did because her proposal amounted to nothing less than robbing the Roman emperor of his personal province of Egypt to move it into the Sassanide sphere of influence. A huge betrayal, particularly as it contradicted everything that her former husband Odenathus stood for. Of course, she was not thinking in terms of betrayal. Her thought was to succeed where Cleopatra had failed, the idea being to move the center of the Roman Empire from Rome to Egypt. Nor did she intend to cave to the Sassanides. On the contrary, she was so confident that she intended to control them and use them as a counterweight to move the empire's center of gravity. It turned out that her basic idea was not so far wrong. Sixty some years later that was what Constantine did, only, instead of moving the center to Egypt, he moved it to Constantinople. This same marriage proposal is the one reported by the Egyptologists as made by the widow of Tutankhamen to the King of the Empire Era Hittites on the pretext that otherwise she would be forced to marry an old man she didn't like. And that is what happened. After the fall of Palmyra, Zenobia was obliged to marry an aged Roman senator. It appears that she is none other than the one known to the Egyptologists as the widow of Tutankhamen, Alexander Severus dead in 236 AD. With her defeat, Rome destroyed the Cleopatra gambit, the scheme of moving the capitol to Egypt. That was the basic achievement of the 19th Dynasty, the House of Constantine.

Ramses II had reddish hair; Constantine had reddish hair. Ramses II died in his seventies as did Constantine. The time from the end of Claudius Gothicus in 270 AD to the end of Constantine in 337 AD is sixty-seven years which is the time the Egyptologists give to the reign of Ramses II. This goes to show how the Egyptians counted reign time. If they liked a king they counted his whole career as his reign and so they gave fifty-four years to Thutmose III, Marcus Aurelius, and sixty-seven to Constantine. Of course this means that the reign of Sety was a regency, time spent in the first part of Ramses II's reign. So the Egyptologists, Brugsch-Bey for instance, who count Sety as regent are correct.

And we are always reminded that Ramses II moved the capitol to the city named after himself, Pi Ramses. That's what Constantine did. He moved the capitol to the city named after himself, Constantinople. It doesn't matter that the Egyptologists mean a move from Memphis to somewhere nearer the coast. What matters is that just here where it can be expected, Ramses II moves the capitol which is what Constantine did.

It is said that Ramses II was heralded as the Great King while he was yet in the womb. This is a first in Egyptology. This sort of heralding also occurs for the first time in Roman history about this time, only, according to Gibbon, it was said of Shapur II born in 309 AD. They set the crown on the belly of his mother. However, since the Egyptologists find this claim for Ramses II, Constantine must have made it though Gibbon doesn't mention it. It should be in the Latin authors somewhere. At any rate, Ramses II claimed to be the King of Kings, a first in Egyptology; and Constantine claimed to be the King of Kings, a first in Roman history.

There are other unique instances common to both Ramses II and Constantine that show them to be the same man. For instance, only of Ramses II is it said that an Egyptian king late in his life made his own daughter a queen. Constantine did the same thing. Some of the Latin authors were scandalized by this as though there were a question of incest, but he could appoint a daughter as coregent as well as a son particularly after he executed his eldest son for treason.

And there is the battle of Qadesh won by Ramses II. I have already shown that this can only be Constantine co-opting as his own the feat of Jonathan Maccabeus, but nobody in his day would have criticized him for this because he did win at least one battle by imitating the courage of his hero. This was the battle of Hadrianople in 323 AD against the rival Caesar Licinius. Gibbon quotes a Latin author to say that Constantine won the contest by a feat that 'can scarcely be paralleled either in poetry or romance... We are assured that the valiant emperor threw himself into the River Hebrus accompanied by only twelve horsemen, and that, by the effort or terror of his invincible arm, he broke, slaughtered and put to flight a host of a hundred and fifty thousand men...'. Gibbon doesn't know what to make of this tale, whether to believe it or not. The only reason he mentions it at all is because the Latin author was always hostile to Constantine and so there must be something to it. He suspects that it might be an embroidered version of some great battle long before and suggests that this might be found in the tale of Krishna and Arjuna in India. He seems not to be aware of the precedent much closer to hand, Jonathan at Qadesh.

This battle of Hadrianople seems to be the only one recorded by the Latin authors that makes Constantine out to be the reincarnation of Jonathan. In fact, of course, it cannot be the battle meant by the Egyptological texts because there at that Qadesh, Ramses II, Constantine, was a young man. He is referred to as the prince. At Hadrianople Constantine was in his sixties and a great deal more than a mere prince. And also, the clincher, Egyptology names his enemy at his Qadesh as Muwatallis II the Empire Era Hittite who is none other than the Sassanide Bahram II who reigned from 276 to 293 AD. That brackets Constantine's battle of Qadesh and this earlier battle, it seems to me, accounts for the obscurities that Gibbon says makes the Latin author's account of Hadrianople hard to follow – that author was either comparing the two battles, Qadesh and Hadrianople, or he confused the two, or later copyists of the Latin author were only too eager to transfer the miracle of Qadesh when Constantine was a pagan to Hadrianople when he was, officially, a Christian. At any rate, the miracle of Hadrianople sounds like the one at Qadesh and we can doubt that Constantine in his sixties managed to pull off the same feat as thirty years before.

When Aurelian destroyed Palmyra in 273 AD he destroyed Rome's outpost against the Sassanides which opened up a vacuum. Into this vacuum poured the Parthian armies and there is no reason why Constantine, an up and comer in the court of Diocletian, would not have stopped them at the chokepoint, at the crossroads of Hazor, Qadesh the Old, in the same way that Jonathan stopped his enemies there more than four hundred years before. It would have been the loss of this battle that drove the Sassanide Narses I to make peace with Rome around the year 293 AD. In previous years the Sassanides were nothing but trouble to Rome and then suddenly they conceive a preoccupation with their east border and only want peace in the west with Rome. The historians don't quite explain this about face but the Egyptologists do – they introduce the deux ex machina, Ramses II, who seemed to be the incarnation of the God of War.

Constantine was a supreme cavalry tactician. The odds didn't matter; he won anyway every time whether against rival Caesars, of which there were many ever since Diocletian split the empire into east and west, or against the Sassanides. No wonder the bishops at Nicea where they drew up the Creed in 325 AD deferred to his judgment since he seemed to be the infallibly victorious King David himself come to Earth again to end paganism and establish Christianity as the religion of empire. So why don't the Egyptologists find Ramses II talking like a Christian? That's because, as Gibbon says, his Christianity was all under the counter. He carried on his government as pagan as usual and was not persuaded until he lay on his deathbed, a last minute conversion. But then of course neither do the Egyptologists find anyone talking like a Christian before Ramses II or afterwards through the 25th Dynasty but that's only because they can't and dare not and maintain their anachronisms at the same time. Christian art first shows up on 19th Dynasty walls. This art is regarded as graffiti put there long after. In fact it was contemporary and can be expected.

It is Merneptah, the son and successor of Ramses II, who gives us the next proof of who is who. Some Egyptologists give him four years. They're right. Constantine II son of Constantine reigned four years from 337 to 341 AD.

And it was Merneptah who for the first time in Egyptology found himself up against the People of the Sea. That's right too. It was Constantine II who first defended Egypt from the Goths who, like the Sassanides, seem to have waited 'til Constantine died before they went on the offensive. From the north shore of the Black Sea they launched their ships to loot and burn their way down the Aegean Coast and into the east Mediterranean. Pictures in old Egyptian texts show them on land with their ox carts. Gibbon mentions those same ox carts that they used when travelling overland. A peculiar thing about these Goths – they claimed they were the lost tribes of Israel returning home. Gibbon views this claim with skepticism, but Merneptah, Constantine II, seems to have taken it seriously. On the Merneptah stele, set up in memorial of his victory over them, he says, as it is translated by the Egyptologists, '...the seed of Israel is not...' This was said in the midst of a recital of defeated tribes. The noun translated as 'seed' means posterity or descendants. The corresponding verb means to leave, depart, to leave one's country, and go into exile. And so the phrase can be translated as '...the exiles of Israel are defeated...' Claudius Gothicus had defeated them for which reason he was given the title Gothicus. Why then don't the People of the Sea appear in his reign in Egyptology, the reign of Ramses I? Because at that time they threatened Italy not Egypt. When that didn't work they retreated east to the Black Sea out of reach of Roman armies, only to bide their time 'til Constantine died. As it turned out, their end at the hands of Merneptah, Constantine II, was highly exaggerated. A few decades later they were back to haunt the reign of Ramses III, Theodosius, and his 20th Dynasty.

Constantine was not a good Christian. He was so brilliant and able that he had no need of God until he lay on his deathbed. Only then did he realize that all was not of his doing. Nor was his brief posterity any better, particularly the last of them, Julian, who was as brilliant in scholarship as his great uncle, Constantine, was on the battlefield. Julian was the one that his followers, the Copts and others in Egypt, marked as starting an era. The only trouble with that is that this era only occurs in Latin history. It does not occur in Egyptology and so it does not occur at all, as far as ancient history is concerned. Julian the Apostate, I am almost sorry to observe, especially since Gibbon gives him so many admirable pages, shows up in Egyptology as Siptah, the last of the 19th Dynasty, the poor fellow with the clubfoot or some kind of deformity. If this is indeed Julian, now we know why they said he could run surprisingly well, the only Roman emperor who made a name for himself that way. What they meant was that he could run well in spite of his deformed foot. He persecuted the Christians which makes me wonder if he was the original drag-footed villain. But a doctor who saw the mummy said that atrophy and shortening of the right leg looks like a case of polio. Siptah's mummy shows the same, or similar discoloration of the skin as does Merneptah's. They both died in battle so I guess this discoloration is from a substance the body was packed in to preserve it during shipment back home. I say they died in battle, I mean Constantine II and Julian, and the mere fact that the two mummies show the same discoloration is some indication of who they are. Gibbon says that Julian died from a thrown spear that hit him in the side and pierced his liver while he was fighting the Sassanides. It may or may not have been in the side. Harris and Weeks don't mention a wound but that doesn't mean it isn't there. I'd look for a wound anywhere on the torso and if it is not apparent I'd expect another sloppy or out of place 'embalmer's' cut of the sort on the mummy of Thutmose IV, Caracalla. Siptah died in his twenties as did Julian. The Egyptologists are puzzled by Siptah's parentage. That's because Julian was the son of one of Constantine's relatives. And the Egyptologists find in the lead-up to Siptah's reign that a certain high official practically ran the country. That's right. Gibbon passes on the old joke from a Latin author that Constantius had some credit with him, that official. Constantius was Constantine's last remaining son, dead in 360 AD, and Julian's immediate predecessor. However, in Egypt, Julian's reign was counted from his brother's death in 356 AD and so Julian reigned for seven years 'til he died in 363 AD. The Egyptologists give Siptah a seven year reign.

And there is the name Siptah, the name itself. It is Greek for Augustus. It is a passable Greek version of the Greek form of the Latin name Augustus. There were a lot of things they could have called Julian besides Apostate which they called him supposedly because he reverted to paganism. While that fits, I have another explanation. It is just the sort of play on words that they did back then. For instance a Ptolemy was called Big Belly and another was called Chick Pea, names that come from word play on their real names. Take the name Siptah. Change the 's' and 'p' around, tack on an 'a' and a 't', and you have Apostate, just the sort of thing that would have amused people at that time. And today too for that matter since the art of wordplay still lives.

So much for the 19th Dynasty that Grimal runs from 1295 to 1188 BC.

CHAPTER TEN

THE EMPIRE ERA HITTITES ARE THE SASSANIDES

THE EGYPTOLOGISTS SAY that Ramses I came to the throne in the time of the Empire Era Hittite Suppiluliumas I. That's right since Ramses I is Claudius Gothicus reigning 268 to 270 AD while this 'Hittite' is the Sassanide Shapur I reigning from 241 to 272 AD. Brugsch-Bey, in his *Egypt Under the Pharaohs*, reads the name of this Hittite as Shapalili, or Saplel, or Saprer, the 'l' and 'r' being interchangeable. With Saprer he very nearly gets it right. The name is Shapur. For this reason, instead of the nonsensical Suppiluliumas I'll use the more correct Saprer. The Egyptologists end him four or five years after the end of Tutankhamen, Alexander Severus dead in 236 AD. That's wrong. It was Shapur's father, Ardishir, who ended then. I suppose the reason they make this mistake is that Shapur did his aged father's fighting for him and so when Ardishir died the Egyptologists assume it was Shapur instead. At any rate, they say that Saprer I suddenly improved the fortunes of the Hittites after the end of the previous dynasty, the Old Kingdom

THE EMPIRE ERA HITTITES ARE THE SASSANIDES

Hittites that had lasted about three hundred years. That's right. Shapur I did that for the Parthians after defeating the Arsacides who had reigned about that long.

The historian O.R. Gurney, in his *The Hittites*, provides us with the Empire Era Hittite succession as it appears in old records and I find the Sassanide succession in the *Encyclopedia Britannica*. With Saprer I as Shapur I to anchor the two lists, this is how they match up with a few sociopolitical details thrown in which I have selected just to show that the one thing is the other.

EMPIRE ERA HITTITES	SASSANIDES
1. Tudhaliyas I	1. ?
2. Hattusilis II	2. ?
3. Tudhaliyas II	3. Sasan
4. Arnuwandas I	4. Babak
5. Tudhaliyas III	5. Ardishir - 208-241 AD
6. Saprer I – He and his father started a Hittite renaissance in the power vacuum of Akhenaten.	6. Shapur I – 241-272 He and his father started a Parthian renaissance in the power vacuum of Heliogabalus
7. Arnuwandas II	7. Hormizd - 272-273
8. Mursilis II	8. Bahram I - 273-276
9. Muwatallis II – He lost the battle that led to the peace treaty	9. Bahram II – 276-293 He lost the battle that led to the peace treaty
10. Urhi-Teshub – He took the throne but was soon evicted by his uncle Hattusilis III	10. Bahram III – 293 He took the throne but was soon evicted by his uncle Narses I
11. Hattusilis III – He was the viceroy in Anatolia. He evicted his nephew and made the peace treaty	11. Narses I – 293-302 He was the viceroy in Anatolia. He evicted his nephew and made the peace treaty
12. Tudhaliyas IV	12. Hormizd II – 302-309
13. Arnuwandas III	13. Narses II – 309
14. Saprer II – After his reign the Empire Era Hittites in Anatolia were ended by the People of the Sea	14. Shapur II – 309-379 After his reign the Sassanides in Anatolia were ended by the Goths

So as not to clutter things up too much I add here separately the matchup of familial relationships of one dynasty with the other, the matchup of the father-son succession of these Hittites with that of the Sassanides. To make things as simple as possible, I refer to the rulers by number rather than by name. Thus instead of saying that Shapur I is the son of Ardishir, I show that ruler number six is the son of ruler number five.

EMPIRE ERA HITTITES	SASSANIDES
1. Son of ?	1. ?
2. Son of ?	2. ?
3. Son of ?	3. Son of ?
4. Son of 3	4. Son of 3
5. Son of 4	5. Son of 4
6. Son of 5	6. Son of 5
7. Son of 6	7. Son of 6
8. Son of 6	8. Son of 6
9. Son of 8	9. Son of 8
10. Son of 9	10. Son of 9
11. Son of 8	11. Son of 8 – the historians say Son of 6
12. Son of 11	12. Son of 11
13. Son of 12	13. Son of 12
14. Son of 12	14. Son of 12

As you can see, the paternity numbers in the one list match those in the other save only in the case of ruler number 11 whom the Hittite list records as son of 8 while the historians say he is son of 6 in the Sassanide version. Hattusilis III, ruler 11, says in the peace treaty that he is the son of Mursilis II, ruler 8. So why don't the historians allow Narses I, ruler 11, to be the son of Bahram I, ruler 8? Apparently because they believe that Narses erased the name of Bahram. And since Bahram I and his predecessor were brothers, sons of 6, Shapur I, the historians assume that Narses was their brother and Shapur's son since any possibility that Ardishir was his father, that Shapur and Narses were brothers, would be a stretch. In other words, the historians are guessing. They do not know for sure who Narses' father was. I can think of at least one scenario where they are right but Gurney's list is right at the same time – suppose that Narses was the son of Shapur but was orphaned and adopted by Bahram I in which case he, Hattusilis III, could say that Mursilis II was his father. Given these obscurities, we could say that Hittite ruler number 11 is the son of 8 or perhaps of 6 and that Sassanide ruler number 11 is the son of 6 or perhaps of 8. In any case, the Sassanide list has been tampered with and so there is every reason to assume that the true paternity of ruler number 11 is the same in both the Hittite and Sassanide lists. In that case we have the Hittite paternity number sequence of '?, ?, ?, 3, 4, 5, 6, 6, 8, 9, 8, 11, 12, 12' and meanwhile the Sassanide sequence is the same.

Incidentally, in ancient times any one name was written differently according to the different script of different nations. For instance, Ardishir in Latin, Abdi Ashirta in Egyptian hieroglyphic, Tushratta in cuneiform and Tudhaliyas in Hittite hieroglyphic, are all the same name. Take Tudhaliyas. The soft 'dh' is 'sh'. The 'l' and 'r' are interchangeable. The 'yas' may as well be 'atta',a superfluous suffix. And so for Tudhaliyas we have Tushratta which is Abdi Ashirta or Ardishir. And the Egyptological Buraburiash, who commiserated with Amenhotep III, Septimius Severus, over his crippled feet, is probably Babak the father of Ardishir. Babak is Babash and the old scribes were only too ready to throw in nonsense consonants so that Babash becomes Buraburiash.

CHAPTER ELEVEN

RAMSES III IS THEODOSIUS

AS FAR AS RECOGNIZABLE MATCHUPS ARE CONCERNED, Dynasties 20 through 25 are a tale soon told. But at least there is enough detail that we don't have to wonder who these people are or at least when they lived. Since the Egyptologists run Dynasties 23 and 24 concurrently with 21 and 22, it would simplify things to set them aside and ignore them. All we have to do to account for things is to pay attention to Dynasties 20, 21, 22 and 25. After the end of the 20th Dynasty of Theodosius around 482 AD, the 21st Dynasty follows in good order to the end of ancient Egypt, about 616 AD when Chosroes invaded. Then, for reasons already explained in the Introduction, the Egyptologists drop back to 293 AD and the beginning of the 22nd Dynasty which ran to about 508 AD if I use Grimal's dynastic length. Then, according to Grimal, the 25th Dynasty started seventeen years earlier which would be 491 AD. However, since Piankhy reads like Clovis, I'll adjust that 491 to 480 AD when Clovis began to reign. So that's the layout of these dynasties as I find it. Now to prove it.

I've already said that Ramses III of the 20th Dynasty

must be Theodosius because it was his dynasty that followed that of Constantine and because the interval between the deaths of Ramses II and Ramses III is the same as that between the deaths of Constantine and Theodosius and because Ramses III battled the People of the Sea the way that Theodosius did the Goths. There are other matchups. For instance, Ramses III began to reign at thirty-three years of age as did Theodosius; he had a passion for agriculture as did Theodosius; and he copied the name, reputation and family names of Ramses II when it was Theodosius who was advised by the priests to imitate the name and reputation of Constantine. And it appears that the record of Ramses III also adopted wholesale a conspiracy that actually occurred in the reign of Ramses II. At any rate this conspiracy which the Egyptologists assume was against Ramses III reads like the one that Gibbon describes as aimed at Constantine who ended it circa 333 AD with executions of relatives and high officials, the same thing the Egyptologists say Ramses III did. But Gibbon mentions no such conspiracy against Theodosius.

There is an explanation for Theodosius' uncritical adoption of things Constantinian – scribes trained in hieroglyphics were usually pagan and these, along with their priesthoods and temples, were so repressed in Theodosius' reign that he probably had no one to write his own records in that monumental script even when he wanted to. I can imagine that the same priests who had urged on the mobs that lynched pagans and wrecked old temples replied to Theodosius' complaint that there was no one left to write in hieroglyphics – 'So? Just copy Constantine's stuff. Who's to know? Nobody reads it anymore anyway'. As the Egyptologists say, the art of hieroglyphics was quickly fading in Theodosius' reign.

But there is a least one matchup involved here of the sort that amounts to proof. Only once in Egyptology, not before and not since, and just here where I expect it, does a ruler go on record as having a passion for breeding and raising chickens. This was a 20th Dynasty Ramesside, apparently Ramses VIII who died about twenty-eight years after the death of his father Ramses III. This is the fingerprint of Honorius as sure as I'm sitting here. It was he who died twenty-eight years after his father Theodosius and he is the only ruler in the annals of Rome to have had a passion for breeding and raising chickens. Gibbon mentions the story that Honorius was deeply concerned at some latest incursion of the barbarians, but only because he feared his chicken farms might be in some danger. He had a rooster named Rome and he thought this might be the one meant in the despatches. It turned out the bird was quite safe; it was only the city that was at risk and so not to worry. The Latin authors, and Gibbon, made fun of him for this but I cannot help thinking that he followed in the agrarian footsteps of his father and only meant to feed his people, fresh eggs and a chicken in every pot, in times of droughts, famines and invasions. I'd like to know if the Rome breed of poultry dates back to poor little Honorius. If it does, I'd reckon his claim to fame is as substantial as that of any other Roman emperor.

It was in his lifetime, in what appears to be March of 411 AD, that the Goths, the Visigoths under Alaric, sounded the trump of the Twelfth Vulture and took the city of Rome. They looted it for six days, paying particular attention to the trophies Titus had brought from Jerusalem three hundred and forty years before. And then, being Christians, they left so as to leave the Lord's Day and the churches in peace. But then they occupied Italy for seven years which they spent carousing, lounging in the shade, while the trembling daughters of Senators served them wine in gem encrusted cups of gold. And then they left for points west, southern France and Spain.

The Twelve Vultures were twelve centuries of 354 day years, the time allotted to the republic and empire of Rome in an old prophecy in a 'worm eaten manuscript' that came to light over four hundred years before in the reign of Augustus. At the expiration of the Twelfth Vulture, the blast of the Gothic trumpets reminded some of Judgment Day. Gibbon says this was 1163 years after the foundation of the city. That is twelve centuries of 354 day years after, apparently, 753 BC. If we don't count the assault in the 4[th]century BC (by Goths!), this was the first of several on the city culminating in the one of circa 475 AD which is usually taken to mark the end of Rome as the capitol of the western empire. The Theodosian line lasted as long as it did, 'til about 482 AD, only because its last rulers took refuge in Ravenna whose swamps and canals discouraged the attempts of the barbarians. I'd like to know just what real evidence there is for any such Ravenna in north Italy, because it occurs to me that the name Ravenna may as well be a western takeoff on the Semitic 'ar avenna, the city of avenna, which can be written as the city of Tanis. Tanis, in the north east delta of Egypt was protected by swamps and canals and it was Tanis that was the capitol of the 21st Dynasty that followed the timid successors of Theodosius.

I won't venture to identify anyone of the 21[st]Dynasty since they hid out there and the Egyptologists don't dig up anything or anybody that is recognizable. Apparently things went from bad to worse, the bad of the Goths to the worse of Chosroes. I will note though that the Egyptologists mention a certain Piankhy in connection with the beginning of this dynasty, not as a ruler but as someone in the background, and I see that for the first ninety-three years of its existence the 21st Dynasty had no foreign policy. So says Grimal. This is the first hint that the 21st and 25th Dynasties started at the same time. The 25th Dynasty lasted ninety-three years and its first ruler was Piankhy. This strong hint though, cautionary of the true state of affairs, flies by the Egyptologists and Grimal unnoticed. We'll get back to that in a minute. Meanwhile, no Egyptologist has ever proven that this 21st Dynasty leads into the 22nd. Of course they haven't proven that because they can't, because the 22nd Dynasty started almost two hundred years before the 21st Dynasty did.

The 22nd Dynasty is fixed on the real time scale by two matchups, two events mentioned by the Egyptologists on the one hand and those very same events mentioned by the Latin authors on the other. The first of these was a great flood, obviously an inrush of the sea, that occurred in the reign of Osorkon II and the second was an extraordinary eclipse that happened, according to the Egyptological record, about thirty-six years later in the reign of the next ruler, Takelot II.

Just about the time when I expect the Egyptologists to mention a destructive flood that is what they do. They read the old Egyptian record to say that in the third year of Osorkon II that sort of flood happened. I know when that was because the Latin authors mention the same thing. Neither the Egyptian record, nor the Latin, mentions any such thing before or since. Only this one time they mention it. Gibbon, copying the Latin authors, starts his twenty-sixth chapter with the event. Says he: 'In the second year of the reign of Valentinian and Valens, on the morning of the twenty-first day of July, the greatest part of the Roman world was shaken by a violent and destructive earthquake. The impression was communicated to the waters; the shores of the Mediterranean were left dry by the sudden retreat of the sea; great quantities of fish were caught with the hand; large vessels were stranded on the mud; and a curious spectator amused his eye... by contemplating the various appearance of valleys and mountains which had never, since the foundation of the globe, been exposed to the sun. But the tide soon returned with the weight of an immense and irresistible deluge, which was severely felt on the coasts of Sicily, of Dalmatia, of Greece and of Egypt; large boats were transported and lodged on the roofs of houses, or at the distance of two miles from the shore; the people, with their habitations, were swept away by the waters; and the city of Alexandria annually commemorated the fatal day on which fifty thousand persons had lost their lives in the inundation'.

This disaster that happened in the third year of Osorkon II happened in the second year of Valentinian which was in 365 AD so far as I can tell. According to Grimal, this year of Osorkon was the seventy-fourth year of the 22nd Dynasty which would start it, with a little adjustment, around 293 AD, about the time the Sassanides made peace with Rome. The sudden introduction of Parthian names here, names from Susa, implies a line of Sassanides. It takes no imagination to see in the name 'Takelot' the biblical 'Tiglath' as in Tiglathpalezer. These Sassanides apparently reigned in the Delta as an ambassadorial or commercial enclave, or as mayors of a city, which represented the interest of the Sassanides. This obscure and foreign dynasty just goes to show how far the Egyptologists are willing to go in order to fill space.

The second matchup serves to confirm the identification

of the 22ⁿᵈ Dynasty's flood as the one of 365 AD. According to Grimal's reign lengths, the eclipse in the fifteenth year of Takelot II would have been about thirty-six years later which would be circa 401 AD. Gibbon does mention an eclipse but he doesn't put a date to it. However, the context of his narrative does allow the possibility that it was in 401 AD that an eclipse occurred that startled the Roman Empire like an omen of doom. I like to think that Grimal might be ten years early and that Gibbon could have assigned a date early in 411 AD just before the trump of the Twelfth Vulture. Now, eclipses were nothing new. So why does this one get special mention in both Egyptology and the annals of Rome unless it heralded that trump? According to Gibbon, it marked the Gotterdammerung of the pagan gods and the usual phenomenon of an eclipse seems to have been amplified by an additional and mysterious prodigy of nature. What might that have been? Volcanic dust blown round the world? The intervening mass of a comet? Whatever it was, Gibbon, taking his cue from the Latin authors, describes the event in very startling terms indeed in his chapter twenty-eight. Says he: 'The ruin of the Pagan religion is described by the sophists as a dreadful and amazing prodigy, which covered the earth with darkness and restored the ancient dominion of chaos and of night'. I cannot imagine a more fitting omen presaging the Gothic trumpets than that the daylight sky over Rome should turn black. By 'sophists' Gibbon means the pagan philosophers, priests and omen-takers, who already expected by reason of the old prophecy some such thing. It was Romulus at his foundation of Rome who conducted the oracle and looked up to behold twelve vultures which he and his posterity interpreted to mean that twelve centuries were given to the city. Alaric and his Visigoths had embraced Christianity and they were delighted to be the ones to bring the prophecy to pass, especially since the loot there for the taking was held by pagans. And so the vision of Romulus came true. Pagan Rome did indeed end in 411 AD. Its conventional end sixty years later was neither here nor there as far as the sophists were concerned.

So, this placement of the 22nd Dynasty that runs it from 293 to circa 500 AD means that the 25th Dynasty started around 480 AD, the same time that the 21st Dynasty began. So now we know why there is a Piankhy in the background of the beginning of the 21st Dynasty and why that dynasty had no foreign policy for the first ninety-three years of its existence. The 25th Dynasty started at the same time, led by Piankhy and lasted for ninety-three years. Of the two concurrent dynasties, the 25th was the senior partner in charge of foreign policy.

And so we have the startling prospect that Piankhy can hardly be anyone else than Clovis, the founder of the Merovingian line of the Franks, the 'Longhaired Kings', whose reputation of a most peculiar sanctity has given rise in modern times to rumors that they had a familial relationship to Jesus himself. However that may be, Clovis reigned for thirty years, from 480 to 510 AD. That is how long Piankhy reigned. Clovis, for the first time in Latin history, introduced chivalry. Discarding the time honored practice of tricks and ambush, he invited his enemy to name the day and the place of battle. Piankhy, for the first time in Egyptology, introduced chivalry. He invited the enemy to bring up his best men and horses in array on the field of battle and then find out which side God favored. In the Egyptological record this God is named Amen, the God of Justice. This is not out of place. It was Clovis' wife, a Christian, who said that before his conversion he worshipped the pagan gods of Greece and of Rome, that is to say, of Egypt.

Clovis would tell his men that one of them would put a thousand of the enemy to flight, a saying from the Bible, the saying of Moses. That was what Piankhy would say. Clovis had a special love for horses. He was guided to a river ford by a hart. He was anointed King with an antique oil of consecration. These same unique things appear in the story of Piankhy. Clovis was called the second Constantine. Piankhy was compared to Ramses II.

I can't say for sure that Clovis invaded the Nile Valley to impose his authority there as 'King of the Romans', the title bestowed on him by the church which it had power to do. There is perhaps no reason why Egyptian scribes might not have scribbled up his records as though what he did in Europe was as well done in Egypt. But on the other hand, there is no reason why he should not have visited Egypt the private province of the Rex Romanorum. The historians have no trouble attacking the Near East with the Goths, the People of the Sea, and invading North Africa with the Vandals under Gaiseric. And so Clovis, who was as powerful as the Goths could as well have invaded Egypt at a time when the East Roman emperor had lost control there. Nor is there any problem with the facts to say that the Church first tried to revive the West Roman Empire with Clovis. The conventional view of course is that this was first done with Charlemagne three hundred years later. I find it particularly appropriate, that just when the church's hopes for the revival of the West Roman Empire were dashed with the failure of the Merovingians, the 25th Dynasty, that is just the dynasty with which the Egyptologists end their version of history.

CHAPTER TWELVE

A CHRONOLOGICAL TABLE

A CHRONOLOGICAL TABLE usually consists of a column of dates and names. While that is good enough for most purposes, it makes it hard to compare one passage of time with another, to see at a glance how big one reign or dynasty is compared to another. And so I have arranged the dynasties of Egypt, Dynasties 1 through 21, like teeth along the shaft of a key. The shaft is the passage of time and the teeth are the passages of the dynasties according to their lengths. And I've done the same with the dynasties of biblical and classical history. The Egyptological key is cut according to Grimal's chronological tables and the standard key is according to the lengths I've explained in the Introduction. Both keys are on the same scale and each shaft is over two thousand years long. You have to look twice to tell them apart.

    The only reason these two keys are not precisely the same, aside from my poor hand at graphic arts, is that the Egyptologists do a lot of guessing. But even so, they've done a good job. Grimal's key is only seventy years longer than the standard one. We don't have to call in a locksmith to tell whether both keys were made for the same lock. It's obvious. The only thing is, one fits better than the other and I've shown you which one that is. Notice that the first six dynasties, Israel, lasted almost as long as the other dynasties put together. Aside from the merits of its signature text, the Old Testament, Israel's duration alone goes a long way towards explaining its extraordinary influence both in ancient times and to this day.

RAMSES III IS THEODOSIUS

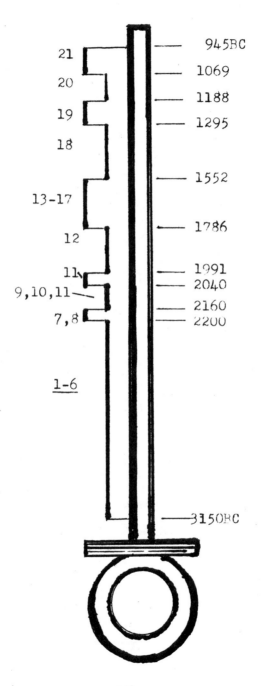

THE REAL HISTORY OF ANCIENT EGYPT

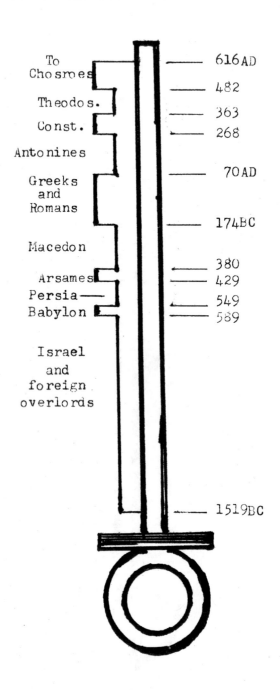

ISBN 1425184618-8